The
Sagebrush
Bohemian

The Sagebrush Bohemian

Mark Twain in California

Nigey Lennon

PARAGON HOUSE
New York

First edition, 1990

Published in the United States by

Paragon House
90 Fifth Avenue
New York, N.Y. 10011

LIBRARY OF CONGRESS CATALOGING-IN-PUBLICATION DATA

Lennon, Nigey, 1954–
The sagebrush Bohemian : Mark Twain in California / by Nigey
Lennon, — 1st ed.
p.   cm.
Includes bibliographical references.
ISBN 1-55778-264-4 (HC) : $18.95
1. Twain, Mark, 1835–1910—Homes and haunts—California.
2. Bohemians—California—History—19th century.   3. California—
Intellectual life—19th century.   4. Authors, American—19th
century—Biography.   5. Journalists—United States—Biography.
6. California—Biography.   I. Title.
PS1334.L47   1990
818'.409—dc20
[B]   90-40448   CIP

The paper used in this publication meets the minimum re-
quirements of American National Standard for Information
Sciences—Permanence of Paper for Printed Library
Materials, ANSI Z39.48-1984.

*This book is dedicated with love
to my husband, Lionel Rolfe—
sort of a modern Mark Twain.*

Contents

Acknowledgments

My appreciation and thanks are due to the following stalwarts for their contributions, material and otherwise, to this book:

To John Ahouse, University of Southern California special collections librarian, for hours of uncomplaining research, photocopying, and delivery service.

To Tony Mostrom, for keeping the faith, not to mention his nose to the grindstone and his shoulder to the wheel.

To Andy DeSalvo of Paragon House, for his patience and his support of my sometimes radical notions.

To Lionel Rolfe, for everything.

To Paul Greenstein, for his valuable suggestions about Civil War and Western historical sources, and for his expertise with wayward jalopies.

To Burbette, Wuzz, and especially the late Moses Jake Burby, for all their work on my manuscript.

And to Larry Haxton and Leith Gordon of The Pines Cafe, Pearblossom, California, for the chicken fried steak that won the West and made it possible for me to finish this book.

What a wee little part of a person's life are his acts and his words! His real life is led in his head, and is known to none but himself. All day long, and every day, the mill of his brain is grinding, and his *thoughts*, not those other things, are his history. His acts and his words are merely the visible, thin crust of his world, with its scattered snow summits and its vacant wastes of water—and they are so trifling a part of his bulk! a mere skin enveloping it. The mass of him is hidden—it and its volcanic fires that toss and boil, and never rest, night nor day. These are his life, and they are not written, and cannot be written. Every day would make a whole book of eighty thousand words—three hundred and sixty five books a year. Biographies are but the clothes and buttons of the man—the biography of the man himself cannot be written.

—Mark Twain's *Autobiography*

Get the facts first, and then you can distort them as much as you like.

—Mark Twain

Preface

I first became aware of Mark Twain, and, hazily, of his intrinsic Westernness, when I was living in London in 1973. My mother, a war bride, had grown up in England, but I was born in California and spent my childhood there and in Arizona, and for me the European experience was like being on Mars. I found the weather uncongenial, the cultural advantages overrated, and the lack of reliable heating and modern sanitary facilities dismal. Had I been a few years older, I might have found some roses amid the thorns, but at eighteen I was still at an age where things like cheeseburgers and Hank Williams rode roughshod over history and philosophy.

That autumn I came down with a pesky virus that chained me to the bed in my unheated bedroom. I was too cold and shaky to get out of bed, so when I saw a battered old book propping up my decrepit bedside table, I seized on it with an almost pathetic avidity.

It was a copy of Mark Twain's *The Innocents Abroad*, his first full-length book (as opposed to *The Celebrated Jumping Frog of Calaveras County*, which was a book comprised of short sketches). *The Innocents* describes Twain's progress through Europe and the Middle East when he was a young barbarian fresh from the wilds of Nevada and California. I had read *Tom Sawyer* and *Huckleberry Finn* as a child, but this was my first exposure to the "adult" Twain. I devoured the book in a few hilarious hours, and as soon as I was on my feet again, I headed for the West Hampstead public library, where there happened to be a five-foot shelf of Routledge and Camden Hotten editions of Twain from the previous century. I checked out as many of them as I could at one time, read them with gusto, and came back for more. By the time I left London I had hidden in my unconscious a vast quantity of half-digested Twain, and when I returned home to Los Angeles and became a free-lance writer, it continued to writhe and seep and seethe like yeast in bread dough. I had never stopped to think that the Mark Twain of *The Innocents Abroad* was, as a brash, uncultured Westerner in Europe, a lot like *I* was when I lived near Covent Garden and the British Museum but could only think longingly of the paradise lost of double-thick milkshakes and central heating. But the intuition was there, some-where, and it was significant.

Some years later I was commissioned by a San Francisco pub-lisher to write a short book on Twain's California years. By then I had long since exhausted Twain's own writing and had been forced to turn to his laundry lists and other scholarly minutiae, and I supposed I was as capable as anyone of composing an entertaining, reasonably factual, narrative of this period of his life. I rolled up my sleeves and went to work.

I had imagined that, given Twain's reputation as "the Lincoln of our literature," someone would have already written a book about his Western period, since it was so formative. I quickly discovered that since his death in 1910 the scholars had pounced on Twain's literary and biographical corpus and had flung the pieces far and wide, covering a great deal of territory, but not the area in which I was interested. Biographers had, it was true, written books, arti-cles, or parts of books and articles about Twain in Nevada, Twain as a San Francisco newspaperman, Twain as a public lecturer, Twain as a public nuisance, Twain and Bret Harte, and so on. But these were, to my way of thinking, unrelated parts of a larger whole. The more I read, the more I became convinced that there were conclusions to be reached about Twain's Western years, and that no one had reached far enough to get at what seemed increasingly obvious to me—the fact that although Mark Twain was born in the Midwest and lived more than half his life in the East, he was a Westerner first and foremost, having spent his formative years in Nevada and California. This was important, I felt, because of the tremendous impact Twain had exerted on nineteenth- and twentieth-century writing and thinking. His blustery, empirical Western spirit had liberated American literature from the parlor politesse of Henry and William James, Edith Wharton, and the like, clearing the path for writers like Jack London and Ernest Hemingway, among others.

As I worked on my research, I noticed a number of consistencies. One was the rather obvious fact that East Coast–based writers, and even Twain's authorized biographer, Albert Bigelow Paine, tended to slight their subject's Western years. They couldn't skip them completely, since Twain became a professional journalist in Nevada, began his formal lecturing career in San Francisco, published his first two books using material gleaned during the time he was based in California, established a national literary reputation from the West Coast, and collected impressions and experiences in Nevada and California that were vital to his later work—but they certainly tried. In Paine's three-volume biography, published in 1912, about three-quarters of one volume of them is devoted to the Western decade. Paine apparently skittered over this material in a rush to get his subject away from the barbaric frontier and safely married in Connecticut. Paine was a thorough and sympathetic biographer, but his plutocratic background made it difficult for him to understand Twain's socio-political legacy as a writer of the people; and his New England sensibility plainly shuddered at the notion of Twain as "the Bohemian from the sagebrush."

Paine's biography remained the standard for a number of years; then Van Wyck Brooks came along in the 1920s with *The Ordeal of Mark Twain*. Brooks was the first of the Twain critics (he was a critic rather than a biographer) to utilize a crude sort of Freudianism on his subject. He reduced Twain to an infantile personality, and accused him of remaining perennially mired in adolescence.

Later biographies were equally caustic. Bernard DeVoto's *Mark Twain in Eruption* was, in my opinion, just Brooks with a little less Freudianism, even though DeVoto had supposedly written it to right the wrongs he imagined Brooks had inflicted on Twain's reputation. I was beginning, however, to notice something fascinating about these critic-biographers of Twain: they seemed to find it impossible to get a grasp on their subject, and wound up using him as a Rorschach test for their own *idées fixe*. Neither Brooks nor DeVoto gave me any new insights into Mark Twain, but I learned enough about *them* from reading their books to conclude that I probably wouldn't want to sit next to either of them on a public conveyance.

Twain's radical nature had always made political conservatives queasy, but in the 1950s Charles Neider came along with a new tactic: subjecting Twain's letters and autobiography to Cold War revisionism. Twain's autobiography had been originally issued in two volumes, edited by Paine, in 1924. In its original version, the *Autobiography* was an essentially political work, containing as much political philosophy as it did memoir. When Neider had done with it, every scrap of political material had been expunged under the guise of "regularizing" the autobiographical chronology. All that was left was a sanitized reminiscence. By the time Neider's bowdlerized edition appeared, the two-volume Paine version was getting harder and harder to find, which meant that for many readers, Neider's revisionist work was the only version available.

In 1966, Justin Kaplan published *Mr. Clemens and Mark Twain*, a biography which began with Twain's courtship of Olivia Langdon and followed him to his grave. Kaplan's premise was that Samuel Clemens and Mark Twain were two distinctly different personalities, and that Clemens adopted the Twain persona to compensate for serious character deficiencies. It was a mean-spirited thesis, but the worst thing about *Mr. Clemens and Mark Twain* was its urbane disregard for anything about Twain, or Clemens, that contradicted Kaplan's notion of his subject's unsavory nature. True to some perverse law of the universe, *Mr. Clemens and Mark Twain* received glowing reviews and became widely accepted as *the* general Twain biography, even though it told nothing about half of his life and mistreated the facts pertinent to the other half.

Mark Twain is certainly not the first author to be abused by his biographers, but in his case there are reasons beyond the obvious ones of author/subject mismatching and literary axe-grinding. As a man, Twain had his failings, but as a writer, he had no peer—in his own time or in ours. Any one book of the magnitude of *Huckleberry Finn* or *A Connecticut Yankee in King Arthur's Court* would have established his literary reputation for posterity, but Twain also wrote *The Prince and the Pauper, Tom Sawyer, Roughing It, Life On the Mississippi, The Innocents Abroad*, and such blazing essays as *What Is Man?* and *Letters From the Earth*. He stood for a universal, and thus completely dangerous, sort of political radicalism—anti-monarchical, anti-imperialist, anti-war, anti-religious, pro-humanist—and this made him very unpopular during the McCarthyite fifties in the United States.

It is my intention in *The Sagebrush Bohemian* to describe Samuel Clemens's *Western* development as an essentially politically motivated writer and thinker. My point is that Twain, coming of age on the Western frontier, was molded into a political animal by a confluence of specifically Western experiences. And just as he received that Western imprint on his own personality, so did he pass it on to the generations of American writers who followed him. Samuel Clemens's journey to Nevada in 1861 to escape the Civil War had far greater implications than he, or anyone else, realized, for it changed not only his life, but the face of American literature forever.

The
Sagebrush
Bohemian

1

The Private War of Samuel Clemens

On the afternoon of August 14, 1861, the Overland stage and the Washoe Zephyr wind both blew into Carson City, Nevada Territory, at about the same time. Rolling up to the Ormsby House, which passed as Carson's best hotel, the stage creaked to a halt amidst a flying curtain of sand, grit, and other frontier impurities, leaving its two passengers to manage their exit in as ceremonious a manner as they could.

As the small crowd lounging in front of the Ormsby House looked on indolently, from the bowels of the coach emerged two rangy roughnecks, hastily slipping into their clothes—for they had spent the past two and a half weeks jolting across the continent in their skivvies. Stretching and yawning, the men—one of whom looked to be in his late thirties, the other perhaps ten years younger—gathered their meager belongings and stood peering expectantly around them for a welcome.

None was forthcoming. From the back of the crowd an appraising comment came: "I thought the governor's secretary was supposed to be on this stage."

"Guess you heard wrong," was the rejoinder from the front of the crowd, and with a few sarcastic chuckles the group began to melt away into the dusty afternoon, drifting past the plaza and the handful of shops and saloons that comprised the capital of the Nevada Territory. Orion Clemens, ever the optimist, turned to his younger brother Samuel and shrugged. "When we've had a bath, they'll recognize us well enough," he observed, trying to hide his disappointment. Samuel, who had expected a brass band and flying bunting, was less convinced, but he kept his sentiments to himself.

Chilly baths poured from tin pails and clean raiment, along with vigorous bushwhacking of obstinate stubble, did indeed transform the two pilgrims into more socially acceptable creatures. Orion then presented himself to Territorial Governor James W. Nye and embarked upon his career as Nye's factotum.

The presence of the brothers Clemens in the Nevada Territory, especially that of Samuel, had to do with the political developments transpiring back in "the States." As has been dinned into the collective literary unconscious, prior to his arrival in Nevada the twenty-seven-year-old Samuel Clemens had been a river boat pilot on the wide Mississippi, and a king among men. He had hoped to follow this career the rest of his days. Actually, his post-mortem description of himself as a "good average St. Louis and New Orleans pilot" held more poetry than truth: in his four years on the Mississippi he had been responsible for two steamboat accidents, one of them serious, and his reputation as a pilot hadn't been particularly brilliant. "Learning the river" required something Clemens would never possess—a methodical, unimaginative mind. But he had soaked up a lifetime of Mississippi lore, and would eventually create a romantic myth of the golden days of antebellum river travel that would more than obliterate his undistinguished record as a pilot.

The outbreak of the Civil War curtailed his career and threw his life into chaos. Samuel Clemens, born November 30, 1835 in Florida, Missouri, was the son of a border state. His parents, John Marshall Clemens and Jane Lampton Clemens, were the impoverished children of Southern aristocracy and themselves slaveowners, and although neither was lacking in humanity, neither saw anything wrong in their actions. Consequently, Samuel, growing up in that environment, saw nothing particularly wrong with the institution of slavery, either. Thus, when Fort Sumter was fired upon in April 1861, and it seemed that all his fellow pilots were choosing sides, Union or Confederate, Samuel had begged leave to ruminate.

"I'll think about it," was his observation at the time. "I'm not very anxious to get up into a glass perch [the pilothouse of a steamboat] and be shot at by either side. I'll go home and reflect on the matter."

Such reflection was cut short by the blockade of the Mississippi River. The prematurely retired Clemens made his way to St. Louis, and thence to Hannibal, his hometown, to visit friends. Here a group of comrades persuaded him to join a small Confederate militia that was forming in the area. Samuel was promptly elected second lieutenant (for some reason there was no first lieutenant), and the fifteen "Marion Rangers" marched forward to "help Governor 'Claib' Jackson repel the invader."

Clemens's career as a militiaman was brief. His fellow Rebels were his age or younger, and they lacked strong leadership; their view of the war, and of their own role in it, was more celebratory than political. Luckily for them, they managed to evade the marauding Yankees during the two weeks their unit was in existence. The worst that happened to Lieutenant Clemens occurred when, during a bivouac in a barn, he fell from a hayloft into the barnyard below, spraining his ankle. He had already begun to suspect that war was not the glorious thing he had at first believed, and this undignified injury, coupled with an even more ignominious boil on his posterior, was "the last straw." His disaffection for military matters had been accompanied by a cooling of his ardor for the Confederate cause. Since there was as yet no formal draft, Twain was able to abandon the militia unit and make his painful way to Keokuk, Iowa, where his brother Orion was living.

He arrived there at a fortuitous time, for Orion had just received the political plum previously mentioned—that of secretaryship to Nevada Territory's Governor James W. Nye. Orion had secured this position through the offices of a boyhood chum, Edward Bates, a newly-appointed member of President Lincoln's cabinet. Although he possessed the necessary political connections, Orion lacked one thing which would enable him to embark on his new career: the funds to get him to the territory. Therefore his prodigal younger brother made Orion an offer he could hardly refuse—he, Sam, would pay for both their passages to Carson City on the Overland. Orion hoped that the change of scenery would wean Sam away from his Rebel cause, and Sam looked forward to a few weeks' vacation in the Wild West.

The two traveled down the Missouri River to St. Joseph, Missouri, where they hunted up the stage office and paid $150 apiece for tickets to Carson City. This sum, incidentally, was a partial payment; Orion also gave the stage company agent an I.O.U. for $100, theoretically collectable in thirty days.

As Samuel Clemens recalled in *Roughing It*, his book about his western experiences, which would be published in 1874, "My brother, the Secretary, took along about four pounds of United States statutes and six pounds of Unabridged Dictionary; for we did not know—poor innocents—that such things could be bought in San Francisco on one day and received in Carson City the next." That dictionary was to cause the greenhorn Overland travelers no end of grief. As the coach left behind the gently rolling country of the Midwest and ventured into rougher terrain, it began flying up and down riverbanks, jumbling the passengers together inside. "First we would all be down in a pile at the forward end of the stage, nearly in a sitting position, and in a second we would shoot to the other end, and stand on our heads," wrote Clemens. "Every time we avalanched from one end of the stage to the other, the Unabridged Dictionary would come too; and every time it came it damaged somebody. One trip it 'barked' the Secretary's elbow; the next trip it hurt me in the stomach, and the third it tilted [their fellow passenger] Bemis's nose up until he could look down his nostrils—he said."

Otherwise, the cross-country trip had gone along well enough through two thousand miles of hostile Indians, rugged badlands, alkali deserts, frontier outposts, and assorted desperadoes. For

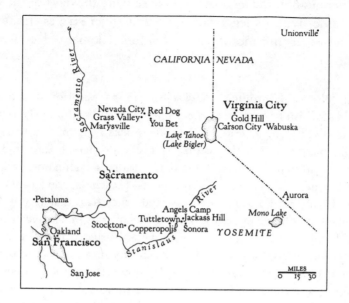

"Twain Country," 1861–1868

Samuel Clemens, who had been born and raised in the Mississippi Valley, the overland journey was a never-ending source of novelty and delight. Every day on the trail brought new wonders, and every mile carried him farther from the turmoil back home and the ruins of his old life. When they finally reached Carson City, twenty days out from "St. Joe," Clemens wrote in *Roughing It*, he and his brother "were not glad, but sorry. It had been a fine pleasure trip; we had fed fat on wonders every day; we were now well accustomed to stage life, and very fond of it; so the idea of coming to a standstill and settling down to a humdrum existence in a village was not agreeable, but on the contrary depressing."

The brothers moved into the Carson City boarding house of Mrs. Margret Murphy, a "worthy French lady" who had known Governor Nye when he was police commissioner of New York City. Mrs. Murphy's "ranch" was full to its balloon-cloth rafters with the coterie of Gotham "heelers" who had followed Nye to the Nevada Territory in the hopes of obtaining sinecures. There was certainly

7

wealth enough in the territory, for these were the days of the Comstock Lode, with its legendary gold and silver strikes. In an early letter home to his mother Jane, Samuel Clemens described the milieu.

> Well, 'Gold Hill' [mining stock] sells at $5,000 per foot, cash down; 'Wild Cat' isn't worth ten cents. The country is fabulously rich in gold, silver, copper, lead, coal, iron, quicksilver, marble, granite, chalk, plaster of Paris [gypsum], thieves, murderers, desperadoes, ladies, children, lawyers, Christians, Indians, Chinamen, Spaniards, gamblers, sharpers, coyotes, poets, preachers, and jackass rabbits. I overheard a gentleman say, the other day, that it was "the damnedest country under the sun," and that comprehensive conception I fully subscribe to. . . . I said we are situated in a flat, sandy desert—true. And surrounded on all sides by such prodigious mountains that when you look disdainfully down [from them] upon the insignificant village of Carson, in that instant you are seized with a burning desire to stretch forth your hand, put the city in your pocket, and walk off with it.
>
> As to churches, I believe they *have* got a Catholic one here, but, like that one the New York fireman spoke of, I believe "they don't *run* her now."

Despite the peristent feeling that wealth was everywhere in the Nevada Territory, Samuel Clemens soon discovered that it wasn't likely to rub off on *him*—at least, not automatically. Orion's secretarial salary was a mere $1800 a year, at a time when the wealth of the Comstock, compounded by the inflation of the Civil War, had driven prices sky-high. A steak dinner in one of Carson's better eateries could cost as much as twenty-five dollars, and only the very wealthy could afford to feed and stable horses. As Samuel wryly remarked some years later, Orion's meager stipend wasn't enough to support the Unabridged Dictionary, let alone provide a sinecure for his younger brother. Orion did employ Sam in various capacities, from stenographer to clerk, whenever he could, but the stigma of nepotism was a constant danger.

The younger Clemens seems to have had considerably greater

practical and business acumen than his brother, for in his *Autobiography* he points out, "Orion was soon very popular with the members of the legislature because they found that whereas they couldn't usually trust each other, nor anybody else, they could trust him. He easily held the belt for honesty in that country, but it didn't do him any good in a pecuniary way because he had no talent for either persuading or scaring legislators. But I was differently situated. . . ." Later, when he had become a reporter on the Virginia City *Territorial Enterprise*, he helped Orion financially by getting the legislature to pass a law "requiring every corporation doing business in the territory to record its charter in full, without skipping a word, in a record to be kept by the Secretary of the Territory—my brother . . . For this record service he was authorized to charge forty cents a folio of one hundred words for making the record; five dollars for furnishing a certificate of each record, and so on . . . Very well, we prospered. The record service paid an average of one thousand dollars a month in gold," he wrote in his *Autobiography*.

Meanwhile, Samuel served as recording secretary and general clerk at the first session of the territorial legislature, earning eight dollars a day. More importantly, during the session he made the acquaintance of politically prominent men, some of whom, such as William Barstow, would figure in his later career. Afterward Samuel took his last few dollars and began traveling around the territory. At first his plans and intentions were vague, extending a day at a time and comprising the most whimsical of itineraries. He knew that the war would soon end, enabling him to return to civilization and resume his steamboat piloting; meanwhile, he could enjoy a pleasure trip through this fantastic wilderness.

First he and a young fellow from Ohio, John Kinney, went to visit Lake Bigler (now known as Lake Tahoe). They had ill-defined notions of perhaps establishing a timber claim along the lakeshore, but spent most of their time floating around the lake in a rowboat or hiking through the virgin forest that surrounded it. One afternoon Clemens, in the process of starting a campfire to cook supper, let escape a spark that leaped across the clearing to a thicket of dry pines. In no time at all he had a roaring conflagration on his hands, engulfing rank after rank of trees in the vicinity until the only safe place for him and his companion was in the rowboat out in the middle of the lake. There they hastily retreated to watch the destruction, sitting there for hours and enjoying the nihilistic thrill of seeing acres of stately redwoods, some of which were thousands of years old, flaming up like tinderboxes. The fire jumped from ridge to ridge, eventually passing out of their sight into the distant ranges. Looking down into the water, Clemens discovered that the glorious picture of destruction was duplicated in the smooth surface of the lake. He found this watery, fiery image to be more beautiful than the reality it was reflecting, for it softened the brutal glare of the flames with an opalescent sheen, transforming the devastation into a transcendental fresco. It evidently didn't occur to him, then or later, that the wholesale destruction of thousands of acres of virgin forest must have had tragic implications; that there was more to the occurrence than the mere opportunity to enjoy a visual barbeque. If such thoughts ever crossed his mind, he seems to have kept them to himself.

Having explored the Nevada Territory to its limits, he could not help seeing the rich strikes being made in the territorial mines. Gradually his interest in precious metals swung from platonic to ardent, and by the beginning of the winter he had to admit to himself that he had contracted the mining fever in earnest. With a small party of other hopefuls he made his way to Unionville in Nevada's Humboldt County, ballyhooed in the frontier press as "the richest mineral region on God's footstool." The trip was certainly educational. Clemens learned to discern pyrite, or "fool's gold," from the genuine item, and how to survive in a "cotton-domestic" tent when the mercury hovered near freezing. His only disappointment lay in the failure to discover instant wealth despite feverish hopes and back-breaking labor.

These lessons came in handy when he moved on to Aurora, which lay in a jurisdictional no man's land between the Nevada Territory and the state of California. Aurora huddled near the summit of the Sierra Nevada, at 7,500 feet. It was a barren, blighted landscape, with weather to match: summer temperatures in the eighties and nineties, and winter lows often plummeting degrees below zero. In a single day the mercury could fluc... forty degrees between morning and evening. Stunted piñon pine trees and juniper bushes dotted the stark mountain slopes, but the prevalent vegetation was the monotonous gray sagebrush, the only plant which seemed to flourish along the Sierra throughout Nevada and California.

Aurora—or Esmeralda, as it had been called by its discoverers—was a bustling boomtown of about two thousand residents, most of them male and single, when Clemens arrived there in late 1861. A steady stream of other would-be millionaires rolled into town daily. There were dozens of solvent silver mines (the largest and richest of which was the Real del Monte), eight rock crushing mills, and hundreds more "wildcat" claims crisscrossing Last Chance Gulch, Silver Hill, and Turkey Hill.

Clemens took up residence in a small cabin on upper Pine Street with Calvin Higbie, a young miner. He had soon created the Clemens Gold and Silver Mining Company, and with his grandiose dreams of wealth his letters back to Orion in Carson City began to take on a tone of hysteria: "Send me $50 or $100, all you can spare." But although Orion was more than willing to bankroll his brother's feverish speculation, his salary was a finite commodity, and eventually Samuel was forced to capitulate to financial reality and accept a ten-dollar-a-week job as a laborer in a quartz mill. Of course he told himself that he was doing this temporarily, and then only so he could observe the milling process firsthand in order to better superintend the activities of his own mining empire when he had established it. Apparently he acquired sufficient information within a week, for at that time he resigned from his position. In the process he also picked up a couple of fringe benefits: a severe chill brought on by the mill's dank conditions, and mild chemical poisoning from exposure to the quicksilver and other noxious substances employed in the refining process. But the worst thing about the job, he wrote in a letter home, was the claustrophobia of confinement, physical and psychological. "It is a confining business, and I will not be confined for love or money," he declared.

SAMUEL CLEMENS, NEWLY ARRIVED IN THE NEVADA TERRITORY, POSED FOR THIS DANDIFIED PORTRAIT IN THE HOPES OF IMPRESSING HIS FRIENDS BACK IN HANNIBAL, MISSOURI.

In *Roughing It*, Clemens recounted a curious tale about Higbie discovering an extension of the Wide West Mine which, if everything had gone according to plan, would have made Higbie and Clemens millionaires. Higbie posted a claim on this "blind lead" of the Wide West, and the two prospectors submerged themselves in a delirious period of dreaming about what they would do with their millions. However, mining law required that some work be done on a claim within thirty days, or the claimants would lose their property. Inexplicably, Higbie (at least according to Clemens's account in *Roughing It*) neglected to work this supposedly wealthy claim, choosing instead to embark on a mineral goose chase for a "cement mine" reputed to lie some thirty miles south, near the vast alkali sink of Mono Lake. Clemens himself ostensibly took a week off to nurse Captain John Nye, brother of Nevada's Territorial governor, who was seriously ill at his ranch nearby. Apparently neither prospector informed the other that he was going out of town. When both finally returned, split seconds too late to "relocate" their claim, they found it in the hands of others who had been watching it eagerly during the thirty-day period. It was to be the first of Clemens's "rags to riches to rags" stories, recounted in *Roughing It*. The records, incidentally, fail to show any claim registered by Clemens or Higbie on a "blind lead" of the Wide West Mine. But as we have seen, Clemens was never overly fussy about minute details.

More likely, the "blind lead" yarn arose from Clemens's embarrassment about the glowing letters he had been sending to his mother Jane and sister Pamela Moffett back home in Missouri—letters assuring them that he would be coming home any day in grand style, a millionaire at the very least. He also provided Orion and his wife Mollie with similar running commentary about the future wealth of the Clemens clan: "I think that by [next summer] some of our claims will be paying handsomely," he had written Mollie Clemens, "and we could have a house fit to live in—and servants to do your work." There is no record that any of his "wildcat" mining claims was ever worth much. Clemens's fate was to watch the few miners become millionaires while the rest, like himself, gained nothing. Yet his dreams of sudden wealth beyond anyone's wildest imaginings persisted. He probably believed these things when he wrote them. But as the months dragged by and he failed to connect with his own personal bonanza, the bleak reality of the situation became unavoidable, and then shame set in. He became morose, believing that he had made such a vainglorious ass of himself that he might never again return home with any sense of honor.

At this stage of the proceedings, Samuel Clemens might very well have been forced to return to Missouri in disgrace, much as he detested the notion, or to throw himself upon his brother's charity, which he detested even more. He knew he could not return to his boyhood home, much as he might have wanted to. But a fortuitous circumstance was looming on the horizon. Samuel Clemens's father, John Marshall Clemens, had been a justice of the peace, and the family was quite literate for its time and place. Samuel himself had always had a way with words, as can be seen from his letters home; before becoming a river boat pilot he had been a journeyman compositor—or typesetter—and had contributed articles to the impoverished Hannibal *Journal* during a period when Orion had served as that paper's publisher. He had also sent chatty travel letters to various newspapers in the Mississippi Valley during his brief sojourns as a compositor in New York and Philadelphia. But Clemens did not consider himself a writer, nor did he regard journalism with much respect. Writing came to him too easily for him to look upon it with anything but amused contempt.

Nonetheless, he enjoyed the glory of seeing his proclamations in print from time to time. After arriving in the Nevada Territory and acquiring sufficient impressions of it, he had sent three travel letters to the Keokuk *Gate City*, as well as a number of letters to the editors of the Virginia City *Territorial Enterprise*. These last were broad burlesques of territorial life written under the pseudonym "Josh," and were well received by the territorial readership, which was quite familiar with their author. Clemens himself evinced some pride in his authorship, writing to Orion in proprietary ire: "Those Enterprise fellows make perfect nonsense of my letters—like all d——d fool printers, they can't follow the punctuation as it is in the manuscript. They have, by this means, made a mass of senseless, d——d stupidity out of my last letter."

One of the pieces published in the *Enterprise* was a parody of a Fourth of July oration delivered in Aurora by a local dignitary, described by Clemens in his *Autobiography* many years after the fact.

> Chief Justice Turner came down there and delivered an oration. I was not present, but I knew his subject and I knew what he would say about it and how he would say it, and that into it he would inject all his pet quotations . . . He had an exceedingly flowery style and I knew how to imitate it . . . I didn't hear his speech, as I have said, but I made a report of it anyway and got in all the pet phrases; and although the burlesque was rather extravagant, it was easily recognizable by the whole Territory as being a smart imitation. It was published in the *Enterprise*, and just in the nick of time to save me. That paper's city editor was going East for three months and by return mail I was offered his place for that interval.

Looking backward and forward over the life of the man who would be known as Mark Twain, one is struck by the number of coincidences and semi-coincidences that marked the climactic points of his history. His own writing is full of descriptions of them. Probably the most important of these coincidences was the confluence of intentions, at the end of July 1862, of Samuel Clemens and Joseph Goodman, editor and publisher of the *Territorial Enterprise*. Clemens had just written to Orion: "I owe about $45 or $50, and have got about $45 in my pocket. But how the hell I am going to live on something over $100 until October or November is singular. The fact is, I must have something to do, and that *shortly*, too . . . Now write to the Sacramento *Union* folks . . . and tell them I'll write as many letters a week as they want for $10 a week. My board must be paid . . . If they want letters from here—who'll run from morning till night collecting material cheaper? . . . Now it has been a long time since I couldn't make my own living, and it shall be a long time before I loaf another year." He had been hoping to correspond for a new paper to be started by William Gillespie, whom he had met in the territorial legislature, but by early July it appeared that the publication was not going to get off the ground.

At precisely that same time, Joseph Goodman was suggesting to his managing editor at the *Enterprise* that the author of the "Josh" screeds should be added to the paper's staff. Clemens's burlesques had, it should be pointed out, little of the flavor even of their author's subsequent *Enterprise* articles; one of them was a portrait of a self-obsessed public lecturer, dubbed "Professor Personal Pronoun." The professor's lecture, according to "Josh," was so egotistical that it couldn't be printed fully—the type cases had been denuded of capital *I*'s before it had been half set. The satirical Fourth of July oration was hardly better, beginning, "I was sired by the Great American Eagle and foaled by a continental dam," and going rapidly downhill from there.

Clumsy as these attempts at levity were, Goodman heard something in them. He was a rather literate gentleman, and in just a few years under his direction the *Enterprise*, formerly a rusty frontier weekly, had grown into a highly successful daily, "printed by steam," with palatial offices and a faithful following. Goodman had accomplished this through his pragmatic understanding of the politics of frontier journalism; he knew, in short, how to back up his editorial judgment with his revolver when the need arose. With this double-barreled policy, he had earned the respect of the roughneck inhabitants of the Territory, so that the *Enterprise* was not only the best-read sheet in Nevada, but was also eagerly perused by readers across the Sierra in San Francisco and Sacramento too.

Samuel Clemens's "Josh" contributions struck the right chord in Goodman, who detected a vein of writing talent in this failed prospector. At the same time, the *Enterprise*'s chief reporter, Dan De Quille (whose real name was William Wright), was planning on taking a much-needed vacation to visit his wife and family "back in the states," and the paper was in need of another hand at the bellows. So Goodman directed his managing editor, William H. Barstow, to dispatch a letter to Clemens, offering him a job as the *Enterprise*'s local reporter at a salary of twenty-five dollars a week—just as Clemens was writing to Orion, practically begging him to contact various newspapers about possible employment.

Clemens had met Barstow during the first session of the Nevada Territorial Legislature, and Barstow had been duly impressed. Indeed, it had been Barstow who initially directed Goodman's attention to Clemens's writing. The letter from the *Enterprise* reached Samuel Clemens in Aurora in midsummer, 1862. Although Clemens later wrote in *Roughing It* that the job offer seemed a godsend, his letters indicate that at first he had serious reservations about accepting it. For one thing, his prospecting fever had not yet broken, even if his budget had. He did not want to admit, even to himself, that his mining career had ended in failure. So despite his poverty, he pondered his future yet awhile longer. He wrote to Orion that he intended to take "a walking trip of 60 or 70 miles through a totally uninhabited country." He had been considering a visit to the White Mountain mining district, which was about that distance from Aurora.

However, he did not make that trip until September. In midsummer, it appears, he may have headed south to inspect the sudden flurry of mining activity in Soledad Canyon, located about fifty miles north of present-day Los Angeles and three hundred miles south of Aurora. In support of this theory, the late Arthur B. Perkins, a California historian, described having seen an entry with Clemens's name, dating from this period, on the registry of the stagecoach hotel at Lyons Station, the closest stage stop to the Soledad Canyon mines. On his travels through the territory, Clemens had heard enthusiastic reports about the booming mining economy of southern California—where the first gold had actually been discovered in 1842, rather than, as popularly believed, at Sutter's Mill in 1848. By 1862 the San Francisco and Nevada newspapers were carrying glowing reports about the huge copper strikes being made in the area, and it is possible that Clemens, always on the alert for new opportunities, could have decided to have a look at "the next big thing." He may have felt, as did numerous others, that the mines in the northeast were becoming played out, and that the better opportunities lay southward.

Wherever he went, he was back in Aurora by the middle of August, and his mind was made up: he would become a reporter. He abandoned the decrepit cabin he had been sharing with his friends Calvin Higbie and Daniel Twing and, unable to afford a horse or stage fare, embarked on a 130-mile hike to Virginia City to begin his journalistic servitude.

The searing summer heat of the Nevada desert was a formidable enemy, so Clemens did his walking by night and spent the days sleeping in haystacks or in whatever brush he could find. On his back he carried a bedroll of heavy woolen army blankets; he had no other possessions besides the faded blue flannel shirt and rough pants he was wearing. When he finally came dragging into the city room of the *Enterprise*'s handsome brick building on C Street, his appearance was truly arresting. He was malodorous with sweat and blanketed with white alkali dust from the trail; he displayed an almost waist-length, matted, reddish brown beard; his slouch hat was caved in and disreputable—but no more so than the rest of his costume; and the evidence of his recent haystack sleeping quarters clung visibly to his clothes. The moment he walked into the city room he unlimbered his bedroll and flung it to the floor— whereupon he collapsed before Joseph Goodman's partner, Denis McCarthy, who was holding down the fort at the moment, and began speaking in such a long, drawn-out drawl that McCarthy wondered if he would ever finish his sentence. Clemens introduced himself thusly: "My starboard leg seems to be unshipped. I'd like about one hundred yards of line; I think I am falling to pieces." Then he added, although not hastily, that he wanted to see Mr. Barstow or Mr. Goodman. "My name is Clemens, and I've come to write for the paper."

Rollin M. Daggett, the *Enterprise*'s assistant editor, later recalled that Clemens "had been living on alkali water and whang leather, with only a sufficient supply of the former for drinking purposes, for several months, and you may imagine his appearance when I first saw him." Clemens was accordingly hustled off to bathe and acquire "a more Christian costume," after which he set in to learn his job from the ground up—an experience he deals with at great length in *Roughing It*.

Virginia City at that time was an excellent place to receive an initiation into the rites of journalism. It has often been claimed that the latter half of the nineteenth century was the golden era of journalism, and in the annals of the *Enterprise* there is more than enough evidence to support that contention. On the frontier the strictures of Eastern society were at most a faint memory; what the vigorous frontier public wanted was bravado, dash, and personal style, not pallid politesse. The modern reader, accustomed to the antiseptic, 'just-the-facts' tone of modern corporate journalism, would in all probability be shocked by the distinctly nonobjective style evinced by Dan De Quille and the future Mark Twain in their individualistic disseminations of the daily news. The line between fact and fantasy was a negligible boundary on the *Enterprise*, as it generally was on all frontier newspapers of the era. Libel laws were virtually nonexistent, and disagreements were generally settled when the party who fancied himself injured appeared in the *Enterprise* city room brandishing his Colt revolver and demanding satisfaction. For a person of Clemens's restless and freedom-loving temperament, this wide-open classroom was the perfect place to nurture his incipient talents; all the more so since at that place and time there was no stigma attached to being a journalist rather than an "author." That sort of snobbery, which thrived in the stuffy salons of New England, could not survive in the open air of the frontier, with its polyglot population and intolerance of pretension, whether real or imagined. Flowery verbiage was acceptable to the Western reader, to a certain extent, but the preferred form of written expression was direct, declamatory, and speech-based. Furthermore, an entire generation of Western authors from Bret Harte to Ambrose Bierce, recognized even by Eastern critics as significant, had devoted a good part of their careers to newspaper writing.

In the early 1860s, during Samuel Clemens's stay, Virginia City was the richest town in the West, perched on "Sun Mountain" (Mount Davidson) above miles of underground tunnels and mine shafts. Often, workers in the third-floor offices of the *Enterprise* would feel their chairs rattle from a dynamite blast in the bowels of the earth hundreds of feet below them. Virginia City was full of contrasts, some of them bitter. Millionaires sipped champagne in D Street mansions furnished with Brussels lace and fine European antiques, while on the flats below stood the countless tents and lean-tos of poor families whose sons went to work in the mines as early as age seven, and whose only source of water was melted snow, when it was available. But this was class struggle with a twist, for a surprising number of Nevada nabobs had started out as poverty-stricken prospectors. The fortunes of John Mackay, James Fair, Sandy Bowers, and others like them provided a glittering ray of hope to the worn and weary men who toiled in the rich men's huge mines while nurturing their own small claims. The wealth of the Comstock Lode was centered on Sun Mountain, and it had almost singlehandedly financed the Union cause in the Civil War. San Francisco, despite all its riches, was merely subservient to Virginia City, the source of its glory.

Mining was the lifeblood of the *Enterprise*'s news columns—mining, and the endless variety of human situations that attended the daily business of prospecting for wealth. In Aurora Clemens had learned the rudiments of mining; here he would observe the effects of potential riches on the lives and minds of men, and work his own literary claim.

When Clemens reported for his first day of work, Joe Goodman, his boss, took him aside and concisely summarized the nuts and bolts of reporting: "Never say 'We learn' so-and-so, or 'It is re-ported,' or 'it is rumored,' or 'We understand' so-and-so, but go to headquarters and get the absolute facts, and then speak out and say 'It *is*' so-and-so. Otherwise, people will not put confidence in your news. Unassailable certainty is the thing that gives a newspaper the firmest and most valuable reputation."

Clemens's first day on the job proved to be highly educational. "I wandered about town questioning everybody, boring everybody, and finding out that nobody knew anything," he wrote.

At the end of five hours my notebook was still barren. I spoke to Mr. Goodman. He said:

"Dan used to make a good thing out of the hay wagons in a dry time when there were no fires or inquests. Are there no hay wagons in from the Truckee? If there are, you might speak of the renewed activity and all that sort of thing, in the hay business, you know. It isn't sensational or exciting, but it fills up and looks businesslike."

I canvassed the city again and found one wretched old hay truck dragging in from the country. But I made affluent use of it. I multiplied it by sixteen, brought it into town from sixteen different directions, made sixteen separate items of it, and got up such another sweat about hay as Virginia City had never seen in the world before. . . .

This was encouraging. Two nonpareil columns had to be filled, and I was getting along. Presently, when things began to look dismal again, a desperado killed a man in a saloon and joy returned once more. I never was so glad over any mere trifle before in my life. I said to the murderer: "Sir, you are a stranger to me, but you have done me a kindness this day which I can never forget. If whole years of gratitude can be to you any slight compensation, they shall be yours. I was in trouble and you have relieved me nobly and at a time when all seemed dark and drear. Count me your friend from this time forth, for I am not a man to forget a favor."

If I did not say that to him I at least felt a sort of itching desire to do it. I wrote up the murder with a hungry attention to details, and when it was finished experienced but one regret—namely, that they had not hanged my benefactor on the spot, so that I could work him up too.

By the end of that first day, Goodman had declared Clemens to be "as good a reporter as Dan"—a recommendation that Clemens found highly encouraging. "With encouragement like that," he wrote, "I felt that I could take my pen and murder all the immigrants on the plains if need be, and the interests of the paper demanded it."

Unbeknownst to himself, Samuel Clemens had just stumbled into his life's work.

2

Mark Twain and the Miscegenation Society

In the 1860s, from Washoe to San Francisco's Barbary Coast the reporters who wrote for the frontier newspapers often found it expedient to employ *noms de plume*—some might say *noms de guerre*. Thus William Wright of the *Territorial Enterprise* was known to the perusing populace as Dan de Quille, and behind him and his fellows stretched a line that went back to John Phoenix and Squibob, and forward to include hicks-gone-uptown such as Artemus Ward. Our boy Sam Clemens, as we have seen, had followed this custom by signing himself "Josh" in his early submissions to the *Enterprise*, but he seems to have recognized early in the game that he required a less nondescript monicker.

The alias that in the 1890s and 1900s would be found blazing forth from boxes of cigars, and which was one day to be duly registered with the U.S. Copyright Office, had its beginnings during Clemens's Mississippi piloting days. In the late 1850s, the columns of the New Orleans *Picayune* all too frequently seemed to ring with the proclamations of one Isaiah Sellers, an old-time pilot who led off his articles with the line "My opinion for the benefit of the citizens of New Orleans," and ended with the signature "Mark Twain." In

A GROUP OF NEVADA TERRITORY JOURNALISTS. MARK TWAIN IS THE SECOND FIGURE FROM THE LEFT WITH HIS ARM ON HIS NEIGHBOR'S SHOULDER; JOSEPH GOODMAN, PUBLISHER OF THE VIRGINIA CITY *TERRITORIAL ENTERPRISE,* HAS THE NUMBER "2" DIRECTLY ABOVE HIS HEAD; STEVE GILLIS IS THIRD FROM THE RIGHT IN THE BOTTOM ROW.

between, "Twain" would sorely try the patience of his ostensible readers with diatribes on the condition of the river, interspersed with recollections of the good old days of "eleven and fifteen." Samuel Clemens, wearying of these manifestoes, composed a satire on Sellers, calling him "Sergeant Fathom" ("mark twain" in the river jargon signified two fathoms, or twelve feet, of water, the shallowest depth a steamboat could negotiate without fear for safety). This farce, which began by describing "our friend Sergeant Fathom, one of the oldest cub pilots on the river, and now on the Railroad Line steamer *Trombone,*" was designed for the amusement of Clemens's pilot friends, but one of them liked it so much that he slipped it to the New Orleans *True Delta,* where it subsequently appeared.

When the original "Mark Twain" read this burlesque, it took the steam right out of his boilers. Sellers was so hurt and humiliated that he vowed he would nevermore edify the people of New Orleans. Apparently, he didn't; Clemens had accomplished his aim.

Twain in Virgina City in 1864 with fellow Washoe journalists
A. J. Simmons (left) and Billy Clagget.

Early in 1863 Clemens, on the staff of the *Enterprise*, learned that Sellers had "gone up the river for good," and he waxed somewhat remorseful. While he was meditating on the subject, lightning struck: here was a virile, declamatory trademark, characteristic of his past life but well-suited to his present one (as a reporter he was often accused of "running aground" on the shoals of objective fact). It was of no further use to its inventor; hadn't been for some time, in fact. His first use of the pen name in print occurred in the *Enterprise* in early February 1863, accompanying an account of the convening of the territorial legislature in Carson City. Few readers at the time were aware of its significance. And in true academic kill-joy fashion, subsequent scholars would quibble with some of the facts involved in the Isaiah Sellers story, claiming that the original "Mark Twain" didn't actually die until a few years after Clemens began using the pseudonym. Clemens himself agreed that he began using the name during his first stint at covering the Nevada Territorial Legislature for the *Enterprise*. "I wrote a weekly letter to the paper," he recalled in his *Autobiography*. "It appeared Sundays, and on Mondays the legislative proceedings were obstructed by the complaints of members as a result. They rose to questions of privilege and answered the criticisms of the correspondent with bitterness, customarily describing him with elaborate and uncomplimentary phrases, for lack of a briefer way. To save their time, I presently began to sign the letters, using the Mississippi leadsman's call, 'Mark Twain' (two fathoms—twelve feet) for this purpose." (Waggish observers who had known Clemens during his Western sojourn would further cloud the nomenclatural exegesis by positing that the handle "Mark Twain" referred to its impoverished subject's bar tab in San Francisco; but we will not pursue this undignified course any further.)

Clemens, or Twain, fit into the *Enterprise* milieu more neatly than he would ever fit anywhere else. Joseph Goodman had seen immediately that this bush-league Juvenal, whose brother was connected with the territorial government, would be an asset to his paper. Clemens's knowledge of the failings and foibles of territorial politicos was astute, even if it was disseminated in a humorous fashion. During his coverage of the territorial legislature, the newly named

Mark Twain was "elected" Speaker of the "Third House," a group of reporters, lawmen, and other questionable types who met in the evenings at a congenial saloon to burlesque the daily proceedings. Clemens's pompous "addresses" and parodies of assorted lawmakers constituted his first experiences in public speaking, and were hilariously received.

Following Dan De Quille's departure, Clemens assumed sole responsibility for the *Enterprise*'s news columns. Joe Goodman had realized early that his new recruit had a constitutional disregard for factuality. Twain seemed to think he owed it to his readers to prevent mundane reality from boring them to death. "To find a petrified man, or break a stranger's leg, or cave an imaginary mine, or discover some dead Indians in a Gold Hill tunnel, or massacre a family at Dutch Nick's, were feats and calamities that *we* never hesitated about devising when the public needed matters of thrilling interest for breakfast," he wrote in a letter to the *Enterprise* from Washington, D.C. a few years later. "The seemingly tranquil ENTERPRISE office was a ghastly factory of slaughter, mutilation and general destruction in those days."

With some shrewdness, Goodman soon began to employ Clemens as a spinner of yarns and fancy sketches rather than a purveyor of pure, unvarnished truth. Twain may have pounded the final nail into the coffin of "objective fact," but Dan De Quille, himself no mean fantasist, had already laid the foundation for Mark Twain's forays into imaginary realms. De Quille's surreal pseudo-scientific subjects included air-conditioned war helmets, magnetic rocks, and an entire mine constructed of roast chicken, with stuffing for galleries and supporting timbers made of drumstick bones.

Early in Clemens's *Enterprise* career came the story of the "Petrified Man," which described the exhumation of a paleolithic citizen from Gravelly Ford in the Humboldt Mining District. According to Twain, "Every limb and feature of the stone mummy was perfect, not even excepting the left leg, which had evidently been a wooden one during the lifetime of the owner—which lifetime, by the way, came to a close about a century ago, in the opinion of a savant who has examined the defunct. The body was in a sitting posture, and leaning against a huge mass of croppings; the attitude was pensive, the right thumb rested against the side of the nose; the left thumb partially supported the chin, the forefinger pressing the inner corner of the eye, and drawing it partly open; the right eye was closed, and the fingers of the right hand spread out. . . ."

The joke was on the world, ultimately. Originally written to embarrass the coroner of Humboldt County, who was notoriously closemouthed with details surrounding deaths in his bailiwick, the "Petrified Man" article was, Twain felt, an obvious satire, "a string of roaring absurdities," from the mummy's wooden leg to his (and the article's) nose-thumbing pose. But so much for credibility versus credulousness: the item was widely reprinted in newspapers across the country, not as a hoax but in dead earnest. When the item appeared, verbatim, in the *Lancet* of London, Clemens no doubt had cause to reconsider the subtleties of irony—a valuable and tempering lesson for this brash young satirist.

But apparently his education still had a distance to go, for his next journalistic hoax was "A Bloody Massacre Near Carson," also known as "The Massacre at Dutch Nick's." In gleeful terms it recounted a gruesome tale of the slaughter of an entire family by its deranged *paterfamilias*, Phillip Hopkins. "About 10 o'clock on Monday evening Hopkins dashed into Carson on horseback, with his throat cut from ear to ear," Twain wrote cheerfully,

> and bearing in his hand a reeking scalp from which the warm, smoking blood was still dripping, and fell in a dying condition in front of the Magnolia Saloon. Hopkins expired in the course of five minutes, without speaking. The long red hair of the scalp he bore marked it as that of Mrs. Hopkins. A number of citizens, headed by Sheriff Gasherie, mounted at once and rode down to Hopkins' house, where a ghastly scene met their gaze. The scalpless corpse of Mrs. Hopkins lay across the threshhold, with her head split open and her right hand almost severed from the wrist. Near her lay the ax with which the murderous deed had been committed. In one of the bedrooms six of the children were found, one in bed and the others scattered about the floor. They were all dead. Their brains had evidently been dashed out with a club, and every mark about them

seemed to have been made with a blunt instrument. The children must have struggled hard for their lives, as articles of their clothing and broken furniture were strewn about the room in the utmost confusion . . .

The unfortunate head of the household, Twain noted in his article, had been driven to his desperate act by the financial ruin of San Francisco's Spring Valley Water Company, in which he had invested heavily. "The newspapers of San Francisco permitted this water company to go on borrowing money and cooking dividends, under cover of which cunning financiers crept out of the tottering concern, leaving the crash to come upon poor and unsuspecting stockholders, without offering to expose the villainy at work. We hope the fearful massacre detailed above may prove the saddest result of their silence," he wrote at the end of the article.

It was the "Petrified Man" all over again, only more so. Certain glaring lapses in factuality having escaped the reading public, they swallowed the bloody Hopkins whole, and his murderous exploits went roaring up and down the Pacific Coast. At last the bewildered Twain recanted, inserting a single line in the *Enterprise*: "I take it all back—Twain." And then the storm truly descended. Officious city editors in every one-horse town west of the Rockies took him to task in print for perpetrating such a foul and grisly hoax. For forty days and forty nights the beleaguered satirist cowered under the flying missiles of accusation and recrimination. Finally the abject Twain humbly sought out Joseph Goodman and offered to throw in the towel. "Oh, Joe, I have ruined your business, and the only reparation I can make is to resign," he sighed. "You can never recover from this blow while I am on the paper."

But the astute Goodman replied, "Nonsense. We can furnish the people with news, but we can't supply them with sense." Twain remained at the *Enterprise*.

Meanwhile, for better or worse, Clemens's reputation was spreading throughout the West like wildfire. His *Enterprise* articles were widely reprinted in other Western periodicals, and other papers expressed an interest in publishing original material by Twain.

During visits to San Francisco (of which he made several during his stay in Virginia City), he attracted offers from the *Golden Era* and the *Morning Call*. He began contributing to both papers. The *Golden Era*, which was the voice of San Francisco's Bohemian literary community, brought Twain to the attention of an intellectually influential group which included nationally famous humorist Artemus Ward.

In late 1863, Ward (the Maine-born Charles F. Browne) was at the apex of his career as a writer and humorist. His tactic was to adopt the persona of an ignorant Midwesterner, a showman whose "wax works and Beests of Pray" were solemnly averred to be pure and moral family entertainment. Browne's highly successful colloquial mangling of orthography and syntax incited a host of imitators, precipitating a rash of pseudo-illiterate doggerel posing as humor. But Ward, the "Genial Showman," was the only truly amusing "phunny phellow" of the genre. Abe Lincoln had opened a famous cabinet meeting by reading from *Artemus Ward: His Book*, before going on to more mundane material—the Emancipation Proclamation.

Ward was in great demand as a lecturer as well. Having taken the East and Midwest by storm, he decided in the autumn of 1863 to undertake a Western lecture tour. Ward's greatest influence as a humorist had been San Francisco's merry prankster of the 1850s, John Phoenix, and Ward wanted to see the region that had produced him. News of his travel plans excited the Bohemian literary community as well as the man in the street. San Francisco theatrical impresario Thomas Maguire offered to book Ward on the West Coast, asking in a telegram, "What will you take for forty nights in California?" Ward's reply flashed across the continent: "Brandy and water." He presented his "Babes in the Woods" lecture to packed houses in California and Nevada, shocking some of his more moral listeners by rambling on with no intention but to amuse rather than instruct. In some of the mining camps where he appeared, he resorted to hiring a brass band and performing popular songs, knowing his audience well.

Ward arrived in Virginia City with a bang just before Christmas.

Mark Twain, who enjoyed Ward's humor, had ballyhooed his arrival in the *Enterprise*. As a former newspaperman and editor, Ward naturally gravitated toward the *Enterprise* and its jolly crew, and he made it his home base during the two weeks he spent in Virginia City. He gave two lectures in Virginia City proper, at Maguire's Opera House, and made additional appearances down the slope in the suburbs of Silver City and Gold Hill. The rest of the time he spent engaged in mammoth revelry with Twain and the recently-returned Dan De Quille—the "Three Saints," as he called the group. Twain, with his astute eye for uplifting influences, made copious mental notes during Ward's visit. He saw how Ward had cleverly used regional humor to build a national following, as well as how Ward—really just a journalist like himself—had created a persona which he then exploited through the double-barreled exposition of lectures and books. In between visits to saloons and hurdy-gurdy houses, Ward also undertook to instruct Twain, who was a year his junior. Apparently Ward felt that Twain had abundant talent, but that in the uncivilized West it was bound to wither and die. As Twain wrote his mother and sister the following week, Ward had told him he should "leave sage-brush obscurity, & journey to New York with him . . . But I preferred not to burst upon the New York public too suddenly & brilliantly, & so I concluded to remain here." Before he left, Ward agreed to mention Twain to the editors of the New York *Sunday Mercury*, which ultimately resulted in the paper's publication of two of Twain's articles.

Ward's success as a lecturer encouraged Twain to make a few stabs in that direction himself. About a month after Ward had left Virginia City, Twain lectured in Carson City at a benefit for Carson's First Presbyterian Church. Though his text has not been preserved for posterity, by all accounts Twain's first public platform appearance was a success. More than two hundred attendees paid a dollar apiece to hear him speak—a larger audience than Artemus Ward had drawn at Maguire's. Twain, of course, had more local notoriety than did Ward, and the locals probably turned out for his lecture out of curiosity, to see if he would lampoon any of *them*.

*　　　*　　　*

The spring of 1864 found Twain in a restless and agitated state. As he observed in *Roughing It*, "I began to get tired of staying in one place so long . . . I wanted to see San Francisco. I wanted to go somewhere. I wanted—I did not know *what* I wanted. I had the 'spring fever' and wanted a change, principally, no doubt."

His *Enterprise* articles had been appearing as reprints in San Francisco and Sacramento papers with some regularity, and he was beginning to gain a reputation outside the Nevada Territory. But although he had come a long way, literally and figuratively, since his departure from Missouri for the frontier nearly three years earlier, he had an equally long way to go. He had proven that he had writing talent, but its magnitude was as yet unimagined; Joe Goodman, in fact, believed that of his two star reporters, Dan De Quille possessed more of the attributes required for literary posterity than did Mark Twain. In Virginia City Twain had certainly been encouraged to give free rein to his opinions, and this freedom had encouraged his growth as a man and as a writer, but his moral sense, while intense, was still embryonic, and not likely to develop much further in his present location.

At this juncture, the specter of the Civil War reappeared in Twain's life in the form of the Sanitary Fund. The Sanitary Fund was the Civil War equivalent of today's Red Cross, an organization devoted to nursing both Union and Confederate wounded. Largely due to the efforts of San Francisco minister Thomas Starr King, significant sums had been sent eastward from California to support the Sanitary Fund on the battle front.

Following King's untimely death, a Nevada Territory resident (and former Hannibal school chum of Samuel Clemens), Reuel C. Gridley, struck the idea of auctioning off a symbolic sack of flour in the little town of Austin, with the proceeds all going to the Sanitary Fund. In a two-day period the proceeds reached the dizzying figure of $4,349.75 in cash, plus property worth many thousands more. The territory was in the midst of "flush times," with its mines and stamp mills and assay offices booming along, and the territorial citizenry seemed intoxicated with the spirit of patriotic charity. Gridley (who possessed Secessionist sympathies) decided to tour the territory with the celebrated flour sack and repeat the auction procedure.

As the Civil War entered its final year, the Nevada Territory was a hotbed of factionalism. In saloons, hurdy-gurdies, hotel lobbies, and the other public places of the Nevada Territory, factional fist fights between Yankees and Rebels were a daily occurrence. The Confederates were in the majority in Virginia City and Carson City, with the Virginia City *Territorial Enterprise*, under the editorship of former New Englander Joseph Goodman, being vehemently pro-Union. Between Goodman and the staunchly Abolitionist Orion, Twain had continued to receive constant lectures on the evils of slavery, but in 1864 his political philosophy was still ambivalent.

On May 16, 1864, the grand tour of the Sanitary Fund flour sack rolled into Gold Hill, a suburb of Virginia City. In the parade heralding the celebrated sack's triumphal entrance was Mark Twain, accompanied by several other *Enterprise* staffers. The Gold Hill *Evening News*, a rival paper, rather snidely observed that "tone was given to the procession by the presence of Gov. Twain and his staff of bibulous reporters, who came in a free carriage, ostensibly for the purpose of taking notes, but in reality in pursuit of free whiskey."

Maybe Twain was celebratorially bibulous. Certainly, he was still rather uncomfortable with the whole issue of the Civil War. In a letter written the next day to his mother and sister he described the political fence-sitting of Reuel Gridley with a hint of derision: "He is a Copperhead [a Northerner who supported the Confederacy], or as he calls himself, 'Union to the backbone, but a Copperhead in sympathies.'" This could very well have been a description of Twain's own border-state schizophrenia.

At any rate, the day after the flour sack arrived in Gold Hill (garnering nearly thirteen thousand dollars, and shaming Gridley's territorial hometown of Austin no end), Twain, apparently still verging on inebriation, wrote an article entitled "How Is It?" The article suggested that the good, Southern-sympathizing ladies of Carson City, who had recently put on a fancy dress ball to raise money for the Sanitary Fund, had actually elected to ship the proceeds to "a Miscegenation Society somewhere in the East." As was the case with his other controversial satires, Twain's intention was probably to make a point, but again, his flat-footed approach to the subject caused his moral to be lost in a chorus of enraged howling.

Twain later admitted, in a letter to his sister-in-law Mollie Clemens (Orion's wife), that he had been drinking when he wrote this attack, and that it had never been intended for print. "[T]hat item . . . slipped into the paper without either my consent or Dan's," he explained.

> We kept that Sanitary spree up for several days, & I wrote & laid that item before Dan when I was not sober (I shall not get drunk again, Mollie,) and said he, 'Is this a joke?' I told him 'Yes.' He said he would not like such a joke as that to be perpetrated upon him, & that it would wound the feelings of the ladies of Carson. He asked me if I wanted to do that, & I said, 'No, of course not.' While we were talking, the manuscript lay on the table, & we forgot it & left it there when we went to the theatre, & I never thought of it again. . . . I suppose the foreman, prospecting for copy, found it, & seeing that it was in my handwriting, thought it was to be published, & carried it off.

Four of the ladies in question promptly fired off a damning epistle to the *Enterprise*, which did what every red-blooded Western journal was supposed to do under the circumstances: it stood behind Twain. The *Enterprise* did not print the ladies' letter, and it also refused to publish a retraction of the offending article. The ladies' complaint finally appeared a week later in the Virginia City *Daily Union*, a rival of the *Enterprise*. The *Union* saw its chance to really wallop the *Enterprise*, and it exacerbated the fray by publishing a couple of articles in rapid succession, pointing out that the scurrilous Twain had been accusing its employees of boasting that they had raised "a certain amount of money for the Sanitary Fund, but had never quite gotten around to paying it into the Fund's coffers."

The *Union* went one step further. Its proprietor, James Laird, and one of its printers, J. W. Wilmington, responded in print to Twain's

THE GREAT FLOUR SACK PROCESSION.

accusations—although they couldn't name him outright, since the original "How Is It?" article had been unsigned. Still, the author was known to everyone; there was no mistaking the tone of that original editorial, or the sensibilities of its author.

Next there followed an exchange of nasty correspondence among Laird, Wilmington, and *Enterprise* compositor (and Twain's bosom buddy) Steve Gillis. In one of these letters Wilmington referred to Twain as "a liar, a poltroon and a puppy," whereupon Gillis countered that "a *contemptible ass and coward* like yourself should only meddle in the affairs of *gentlemen* when called upon to do so."

Meanwhile, the *Enterprise* was only too happy to publish all this correspondence in full. Twain also attempted to apologize to the wronged ladies of Carson. The title of the ostensible apology was "Miscegenation," and that alone would seem to indicate that his apology was not as humble and contrite as one might have wished it to be. "We published a rumor, the other day," it said, "that the moneys collected at the Carson Fancy Dress Ball were to be diverted from the Sanitary Fund and sent forward to aid a 'miscegenation' or some other Society in the East. We also stated that the rumor was a hoax. And it was—we were perfectly right. However, four ladies are offended." Although he went on to ask the ladies' forgiveness, he added that "We have noticed one thing in this whole business— and also in many an instance which has gone before it—and that is, that we resemble the majority of our species in the respect that we are very apt to get entirely in the wrong, even when there is no seeming necessity for it; but to offset this vice, we claim one of the virtues of our species, which is that we are ready to repair such wrongs when we discover them."

His left-handed apology was not accepted, and it appeared that the matter could only be resolved on the field of honor. Academic experts have long debated whether an actual duel was fought, but Twain kept the story alive in his *Autobiography*. He claimed that he was not anxious to participate in the code duello, reminding his comrades that his marksmanship had its little discrepancies, but "the boys" would have none of it. "All our boys—the editors—were in our office, 'helping' me in the dismal business, and telling about duels, and discussing the code with a lot of aged ruffians who had had experience in such things, and altogether there was a loving interest taken in the matter, which made me unspeakably uncomfortable," Twain recalled some years later. But as Twain, goaded on by "the boys," sent challenge after challenge to Laird, and Laird failed to respond, Twain began to feel bloodthirsty. "The more he did not want to fight, the bloodthirstier I became," said Twain. "But at last the man's tone changed. He appeared to be waking up. It was becoming apparent that he was going to fight me, after all. Our boys were exultant. I was not, though I tried to be."

Five A.M. on the morning of the duel found Steve Gillis (who was to act as Twain's second), Joe Goodman, Rollin Daggett, and other *Enterprise* stalwarts out practicing up their woozy colleague. A nearby barn door had a fence rail leaning against it, and that fence rail was a symbolic effigy of James Laird. Twain soon made the rather painful discovery that he was unable to hit the barn door broadside from a distance of five feet. Finally the compact, peppery Steve Gillis (who was rumored to weigh ninety-five pounds when sodden with alcohol and attired in his customary frock coat, derby hat, pegged pants, and pointy-toed boots) snatched Twain's pistol away from him. By way of demonstration, he blazed away at an unsuspecting sparrow that happened to be flying overhead, and nearly shot the bird's head off. He pressed the smoking gun back into Twain's shaking hand and facetiously congratulated him on his "great" shot.

Just at that moment, Laird and *his* supporters came marching staunchly onto the scene. They had heard the sound of gunfire and had surmised that Twain and company were getting in some practice. They saw the sparrow's last gasp, but did not arrive in time to ascertain who its murderer was. So Laird demanded to know who had done the dirty deed, and Steve Gillis promptly gave the credit to Twain. Wilmington, Laird's second, immediately wanted to know how far off the bird had been. "Oh, not far—about thirty yards," Gillis replied blandly.

"How often can Clemens hit his mark?" was the next question.

"Oh, about four times out of five," Gillis lied nonchalantly. At that, Laird gathered his fellows about him and beat a hasty retreat from the field. A little later that day, Twain received a note from Laird, written in a very shaky hand, declining the honor of fighting any sort of duel whatsoever with the *Enterprise*'s expert on miscegenation.

Twain's next letter to his brother Orion began, "Send me two hundred dollars *if you can spare it comfortably.* However, never mind— you can send it to San Francisco if you prefer. Steve & I are going to the States. We leave Sunday morning per Henness Pass. Say nothing about it, of course. We are not afraid of the grand jury, but Washoe has long since grown irksome to us, & we want to leave it anyhow."

Mark Twain and Steve Gillis were on the stage to San Francisco within twenty-four hours of the aborted duel. The sending and carrying of challenges had just recently been made a rather serious crime, one punishable by two years in prison, by fiat of territorial governor Nye. Since both Twain and Gillis were well-known figures in the territory, it was likely that Nye would feel obliged to make a public example of them. For that reason the Henness Pass route to San Francisco had been chosen, as it circumvented Carson City, the territorial capital.

Behind drawn blinds, the pair tore out of Virginia City and headed over the Sierra Nevada towards San Francisco, where Twain was subsequently to stumble into his rendezvous with literary destiny. His *Enterprise* days had given him a useful trade; in California he would, albeit gropingly, begin to make something of himself at last.

3

Clemens Gets the "Call"

As Mark Twain galloped across the Sierra toward his new life, the *Enterprise* was mourning its loss—after a fashion. "Mark Twain," observed the paper in a sentimental item only slightly tainted with sarcasm (and probably penned by Dan De Quille), "has abdicated the local column of the *Enterprise*, where by the grace of Cheek, he so long reigned Monarch of Mining Items, Detailer of Events, Prince of Platitudes, Chief of Biographers, Expounder of Unwritten Law, Puffer of Wildcat, Profaner of Divinity, Detractor of Merit, Flatterer of Power, Recorder of Stage Arrivals, Pack Trains, Hay Wagons, and Things in General." This obituary went on to add that Twain would "not be likely to shock the sensibilities of San Francisco long. The ordinances against nuisances are stringently enforced in that city." The Gold Hill *News* was less cordial.

> Among the few immortal names of the departed—that is, those who departed yesterday per California stage—we notice that of Mark Twain. We don't wonder; Mark Twain's beard is full of dirt, and his face is black before the people of Washoe. Giving way to the idiosyncratic eccentricities of an erratic mind, Mark has indulged in the

game infernal—in short, "played hell." Shifting the locale of his tales of fiction from the Forest of Dutch Nick's to Carson City; the dramatis personae thereof from the Hopkins family to the fair Ladies of the Sanitary Fair; and the plot thereof from murder to miscegenation—he slopped. The indignation aroused by his enormities has been too crushing to be borne by living man, though sheathed with the brass and triple cheek of Mark Twain.

San Francisco was already on somewhat intimate terms with Twain at the time he took up residence there. He had made the journey over the mountains from Washoe to the Golden Gate on two or three prior occasions, and had sent back articles to the *Enterprise* describing his impressions of the bustling metropolis that was both a suburb of the Comstock Lode and the final destination for Nevada speculators who struck it rich. Nevada looked to San Francisco in matters of culture and civilization, while San Francisco welcomed the Washoe mining nabobs with open arms, since the city's simmering fleshpots were chiefly fueled by Comstock wealth.

Although Twain had harbored some ambivalent feelings toward California as a state ("how I *hate* everything that looks, or tastes, or smells like California!" he had written his mother and sister about a year earlier), he was soon soothed by the sybaritic pleasures life offered in the city of San Francisco. In another early letter, written while he was in San Francisco on *Enterprise* business, he even admitted, "How I do hate to go back to Washoe!" About a month after he became a permanent resident, he delineated the seductions of life in his new home in an article written for the *Enterprise* and reprinted in the San Francisco *Golden Era.*

To a Christian who has toiled months and months in Washoe, whose hair bristles from a bed of sand, and whose soul is caked with the cement of alkali dust; whose nostrils know of no perfume but the rank odor of the sagebrush—and whose eyes know no landscape but the barren mountains and desolate plains; where the wind blows, and the sun blisters, and the broken spirit of the contrite heart finds joy and peace only in Limberger cheese and lager beer—unto such a Christian, verily the Occidental Hotel [in San Francisco] is Heaven on the half shell. He may even secretly consider it to be heaven on the entire shell, but his religion teaches a sound Washoe Christian that it would be sacrilege to say it.

In Twain's opinion, "the birds, and the flowers, and the Chinamen, and the winds, and the sunshine, and all the things that go to make life happy, are present in San Francisco to-day, just as they are all days in the year."

When Twain arrived in San Francisco that May of 1864, he had with him a large trunk half full of miscellaneous mining stock he had acquired during his *Enterprise* days. In Nevada his first crude attempts at striking it rich by plying pick and shovel in mining claims had rapidly matured into a more sophisticated *modus operandi* of speculation in mining stocks. Part of the reason he was glad to leave the Nevada Territory for California was because the territory was threatening, at any minute, to metamorphose into a full-blown state. This change in status, it was generally believed, would have a pronounced effect on the mining stock market and its regulation. Twain reasoned that the stocks he held, especially some valuable Hale and Norcross shares which he had purchased on a "margin," would appreciate considerably before the bottom finally dropped out, as it was likely to do. He intended to sell them when their value was the highest and then live a millionaire's life in a Nob Hill mansion, or take a trip to New York and then rejoin his family in Missouri—the glorious return of the prodigal son. This entire process, he seemed to believe, would take a month at the longest.

The last thing he wanted to do was continue his servitude as a journalistic wage slave. He had enjoyed his *Enterprise* days, but it was his intention to pursue a career as a gentleman of leisure, not prolong his misery as a toiling minion in some dingy editorial office. Nonetheless, his Hale and Norcross stock, unsold, was not going to pay his board bill while he awaited just the right moment to sell it. Thus, after spending the best part of two weeks in "butterfly idleness," as he phrased it, staying at the opulent Occidental Hotel and sallying forth, dressed to the teeth, to the town's gilded palaces of amusement (he even attended the opera, or so he main-

Bradley & Rulofson, S. F., Cal.

PATENT APPLIED FOR

A PORTRAIT OF TWAIN TAKEN IN SAN FRANCISCO FOR USE ON HIS VISITING CARD.

tained in *Roughing It*), Twain found himself obliged to take a reporter's job on the San Francisco *Morning Call*. At the same time, Steve Gillis also went to work for the *Call* as a compositor.

Twain had been offered a position on the *Call* nine months earlier, after contributing a series of articles to the paper which set forth "the condition of matters and things in Silverland" for San Francisco readers. Although in *Roughing It* he makes it seem as though his chief reason for leaving Virginia City was the Sanitary Fund fiasco, Twain's departure probably had more to do with Dan De Quille's return to the *Enterprise* after a nine-month absence. Moreover, he truly was bored with the provinciality of the Territory. As he had discovered in his previous visits, San Francisco was the cultural and literary capital of the West, with scores of literary journals such as the *Golden Era*. During his *Enterprise* days he had received a fair amount of advice like that from Artemus Ward to "leave sagebrush obscurity" and attempt to cultivate a wider audience. So why not enjoy the pleasures of civilization while tending his literary stewpot and waiting for his mining fortune to arrive?

He showed up for his first day of work at the *Call*'s brick office building at 617 Commercial Street on Monday, June 6. His position was known rather pejoratively in journalistic lingo as "lokulitems" (local items), meaning that he was responsible for gathering all of the local news and writing it up for publication. This included everything from police court matters to coverage of plays and concerts, with just about anything in between. Frankly—and Twain himself was undoubtedly well aware of the fact—the job was a step down from the *Enterprise* position, entailing long and irregular hours and little glory; he received no byline on his stories, and the items themselves were short and their subjects often resoundingly prosaic. The *Call* had added him to its staff because its publisher, George Barnes, knew that as "the cheapest paper in California" (its price was one bit, or 12½ cents, per week), it needed "tone" in its coverage of local news. The arrangement would eventually prove less than ideal for both sides.

Twain's work "day" soon took on a wearying regularity: he was at his desk by about ten A.M.; then over at the police court, checking the blotter for incidents; and after that pounding his regular news beats for any scraps he might glean. In the evenings he visited the theaters, one after another, then went back to the office to write up his items in time for the paper's two A.M. deadline. In short, Twain was the *Call*'s general assignment reporter, beat reporter, and re-write man, all for forty dollars a week. He would later explain, with thinly disguised irritation, that George Barnes, his boss, figured there was enough work for one and a half reporters, but not two. "It was awful drudgery for a lazy man, and I was born lazy," he admitted in his *Autobiography* many years later, as if he still recalled his weariness all too well.

Worse for the freewheeling prankster who had perpetrated the Petrified Man hoax on a credulous public was the fact that the *Call* frowned on reportorial excess. It preferred a steady diet of news items, as Twain put it, about "the squabbles of the night before . . . usually between Irishmen and Irishmen, and Chinamen and China-men, with now and then a squabble between the two races for a change." This policy no doubt sprung from the fact that the *Call* prided itself on being "the washerwoman's paper," the daily with the biggest circulation in San Francisco. In 1864, when Twain assumed his duties there, the paper had already been in existence for eight years. Despite its circulation, it knew its place (why else would it skimp on the size of its staff?). It could not afford to join the telegraphic combine cornered by more successful San Francisco journals such as the *Alta California* and the *Bulletin*, even though telegraphic lines had been laid in 1861. With such poor links to national news developments, the *Call* was obliged to make a virtue of a necessity by placing more emphasis on local news—or on its reporter's ingenuity in gathering same.

For this reason alone, Twain's job as the *Call*'s lokulitems would probably have been more than any one reporter could have handled—let alone a reporter with Twain's idiosyncratic work habits. On the *Enterprise*, Twain had developed a tendency to leave his information-gathering unaccomplished until the last possible minute, and would then attempt to fill in any factual gaps with flashy writing in order to meet his deadline. On the *Call*, he wrote in his *Autobiography*, "we raked the town from end to end," gathering "such material as we might, wherewith to fill our required columns—and if there were no fires to report we started some."

This tendency became ever more pronounced during the four months Twain spent toiling in the *Call*'s dreary offices. As the novelty of his new position wore off, he became correspondingly more sluggish and disinterested. His chief complaint, besides the fact that the hours were long, was that he was allowed almost no latitude in his writing. Whenever he threatened to overstep the bounds of quotidian factuality, he heard from George Barnes.

Twain's opinions were unwelcome in the *Call*'s news columns for precisely the same reason they had been welcomed by Joseph Goodman in the Virginia City *Enterprise*: demographics. George Barnes considered his average reader to be a lower-middle-class Irish washerwoman, and insisted that the *Call* unabashedly pander to her supposed taste in reading matter by slanting all material along the most mundane lines. Goodman, on the other hand, had essentially edited the *Enterprise* for readers like himself—independent-minded, irreverent, and above all possessed of a sense of humor. San Francisco may have been more "civilized" than Washoe, but Samuel Clemens soon began to chafe under the *Call*'s socio-journalistic restrictions.

Despite Twain's growing reservations about the *Call* and his duties thereon, he maintained a fairly good relationship with Barnes. Twain seems to have respected Barnes as a human being if not as an editor. For his part, Barnes was fond of Twain and saw real, if undisciplined, talent in him, but privately he doubted that his new employee was cut out for the grueling routine of a "lokulitems." In his memoirs, Barnes recalled that Twain fell far short of fulfilling his obligations as itemizer of local news because he was so intolerably slow in getting around his news beat, and even slower when it came to writing up the information.

Despite all its annoyances, however, Twain realized that his job had some points to recommend it. "No other occupation," he was later to write of his *Call* days, "brings a man into such familiar sociable relations with all grades and classes of people . . . Why, I breakfasted almost every morning with the Governor, dined with the principal clergyman, and slept in the station house."

Twain's familiarity, and his fascination, with the jailhouse and police courts of San Francisco, were considerable. He spent a good part of his working day prowling the station house and ascertaining what cases were on the docket for the police court. The city jail consisted of a line of dim cells in the basement of San Francisco City Hall on Kearny Street. The prisoners in the cells, brought in on charges ranging from public drunkenness to murder, often remained there for as long as a week before going to trial upstairs in the police courtroom. From there, they were shipped to San Quentin or to the county prison, which was located on Broadway above Kearny Street. Conditions at the county prison were cramped and squalid, with several inmates often crammed into a single five-by-twelve-foot cell.

The city jail was almost always full of prisoners with interesting stories. It did not take Twain long to recognize the regular cast of characters in the lockup—indigents, drunks, prostitutes, and other members of society's underclass. In his *Call* items he often turned to the subject of wayward women, such as the charming Anna Jakes.

> Anna Jakes, drunk and disorderly, but excessively cheerful, made her first appearance in the City Prison last night, and made the dreary vaults ring with music. It was of the distorted, hifalutin kind, and she evidently considered herself an opera sharp of some consequence . . . Anna Jakes says she is a highly respectable young married lady, with a husband in the Boise country; that she has been sumptuously reared and expensively educated; that her impulses are good and her instincts refined; that she taught school a long time in the city of New York, and is an accomplished musician; and finally, that her sister got married last Sunday night, and she got drunk to do honor to the occasion—and with a persistency that is a credit to one of such small experience, she has been on a terrific bender ever since.

Twain undoubtedly had his own ideas about the police themselves, but he was not allowed to air them in the columns of the "washerwoman's paper." In one article he rather mildly held up an

S.F.P.D. officer named Forner for censure, inasmuch as Forner had been taken to court on charges of assault and battery. "From the testimony it appeared that Forner had had an arrest of two persons and then delivered them to the care of another officer," he wrote. "While the latter officer was taking the men to the Station house, the plaintiff went up to one of the prisoners to speak to him concerning his bail, when, as he alleges, Forner took him by the collar, pushed him away, and struck him. The Judge remarked that officers must not go beyond the law in the discharge of their duties. It was not unfrequently the case that they displayed abundant zeal concerning arrests that were wholly unjustifiable, alluding more particularly to their making arrests without a warrant, on the mere say-so of outside parties."

One of the two men arrested in this incident was Lewis P. Ward, a compositor on the *Alta California* and a bosom buddy of Twain and Steve Gillis. "Little" Ward, as he was called, was small in stature, athletic, of good cheer, and, like Gillis, somewhat inclined toward barroom brawling. He remained on friendly terms with Twain until 1903, when financial reverses and mental instablity drove him to suicide. It is interesting to note that even though Ward was a close friend, Twain restrained himself when describing his unwarranted treatment at the hands of the police. In light of later developments, it is likely that this restraint had more to do with the *Call*'s political party line than with Twain's own views; but the pressure on Twain to "cramp himself down" must have been considerable.

He relieved this pressure in other ways. One afternoon he was wandering around, looking for grist for the news mill, when he spotted a large, burly constable propped up against a lamppost on a street corner, fast asleep on his beat. Twain immediately rushed to a nearby greengrocer's stand and seized the largest cabbage leaf he could find. He then proceeded back to the snoring policeman's alfresco boudoir, and began fanning him solicitously with the cabbage leaf. He abandoned his post only when a large crowd had gathered around, nudging one another and smirking. The next day the story was all over town that Mark Twain had caught one of San Francisco's finest asleep on the job.

*   *   *

In his domestic life, the ennervated lokulitems sometimes found relief from mundane care—and sometimes didn't. His roommate was Steve Gillis, perpetrator of a thousand practical jokes and, it seems, a true *bon vivant*. In a letter to Dan De Quille, Twain offered a charming second-hand picture of life with Gillis.

> Steve and I have moved our lodgings. Steve did not tell his folks he had moved, and the other day his father went to our room, and finding it locked, he hunted up the old landlady (Frenchwoman,) and asked her where those young men were. She didn't know who he was, and she got her gun off without mincing matters. Said she—"They are gone, thank God—and I hope I may never see them again. I did not know anything about them, or they never should have entered this house. Do you know, Sir, (dropping her voice to a ghastly confidential tone,) they were a couple of desperate characters from Washoe—gamblers and murderers of the very worst description! I never saw such a countenance as the smallest one had on him. They just took the premises, and lorded it over everything—they didn't care a snap for the rules of the house. One night when they were carrying on in their room with some more roughs, my husband went up to remonstrate with them, and that small man told him to take his head out of the door (pointing a revolver,) because he wanted to shoot in that direction. O, I never saw such creatures. Their room was never vacant long enough to be cleaned up—one of them always went to bed at dark and got up at sunrise, and the other went to bed at sunrise and got up at dark—and if the chamberman disturbed them they would just set up in bed and level a pistol at him and tell him to get scarce! They used to bring loads of beer bottles up at midnight, and get drunk, and shout and fire off their pistols in the room, and throw their empty bottles out of the window at the Chinamen below. You'd hear them count 'One—two—three—fire!' and then you'd hear the bottles crash on the China roofs and see the poor Chinamen scatter like flies. O, it was dreadful! They kept a nasty foreign sword and any number of revolvers and bowie knives in their room, and I know that small one must have murdered lots of people. They always had women running to their room—sometimes in broad daylight— bless you, *they* didn't care. They had no respect for God, man, or the devil. Yes, Sir, they are gone, and the good God was kind to me when he sent them away!"

Allowing some latitude for literary embroidery on Twain's part this was probably a reasonable facsimile of the domestic bliss of Twain and Gillis.

Because they tended to be abroad by night and asleep by day, Twain and Gillis, perhaps ironically, required lodgings that were peaceful and quiet. These, it would seem, were not easy to find, for the two roommates were always moving. Tinkling pianos, barking dogs, and boisterous children drove them from one rooming house to another. In some of Twain's letters from this period, such as the one above, there is a thinly disguised sneer at conventional domestic morality. Himself rootless in a far-flung locale, beyond the reach of the ministering hand of any female relative, Twain seemed determined to make the most of his bachelor existence. For instance, in a letter to his mother he made rather calculated fun of her constant advice to him to keep in good physical shape.

> My Dear Mother—You have portrayed to me so often and so earnestly the benefit of taking frequent exercise, that I know it will please you to learn that I belong to the San F. Olympic Club, whose gymnasium is one of the largest and best appointed in the United States. I am glad, now, that you put me in the notion of it, Ma, because if you had not, I never would have thought of it myself. I think it nothing but right to give you the whole credit of it. It has been a great blessing to me. I feel like a new man. I sleep better, I have a healthier appetite, my intellect is clearer, and I have become so strong and hearty that I fully believe twenty years have been added to my life. I feel as if I ought to be very well satisfied with this result, when I reflect that I never was in that gymnasium but once in my life, and that was over three months ago.

Probably Twain had been at the Olympic Club to witness the athletic feats of "Little" Ward, who was famous for his gymnastics and fencing skills. Given his work schedule, erratic hours, and general aversion to physical exertion, he was an unlikely candidate for sports. In fact, his friends claimed that his "exercising was confined to studying up jokes to play on his fellow [club] members."

For awhile Twain and Gillis lived in the Minna Street boarding house run by Steve's father, Angus Gillis. In an interview with the *Call* some forty years later, Steve remembered that during this period Twain was engrossed in learning French. "Mark was the laziest man I ever knew in my life, physically. Mentally he was the hardest worker I ever knew . . . I never knew Sam Clemens to be without a book to study. All the time we roomed together in San Francisco it was generally a French grammar or primer . . . The French grammar went to bed with him every night and often he would wrestle with it until three or four o'clock in the morning. It was not easy for him, but he was a stayer and he was not afraid to practice what he had learned. He used to hunt up the restaurants where they had French waiters and practice on them."

Chez Gillis, Twain also "practiced" another art of which he had always been inordinately fond: composing doggerel. For the album of Mary Elizabeth, Steve's baby sister, he created the following questionable opus based on Poe's "The Raven":

The Mysterious Chinaman

Once upon a morning dreary, while I pondered, weak and weary,
Over many a quaint and curious shirt that me and Steve has wore,
While I was stretching, yawning, gaping, suddenly there came a
   tapping,
As of some one gently rapping, rapping at my chamber door—
"I guess it's Maim," I muttered, "tapping at the chamber door—
     At least it's she, if nothing more."

Presently my soul grew stronger—hesitating then no longer,
"Maim," I said, "or Fannie, truly your forgiveness I implore;
But the fact is, I was washing, and so gently you came sloshing,
And so faintly you came sloshing, sloshing round my chamber door,
That I scarce was sure I heard you—" here I opened wide the door—
     Chung was there—and nothing more!

Then this leathery wretch beguiling my sad fancy into smiling,
By the grave and stern decorum of the countenance he bore—

"Though thy crest be shorn and shaven, thou," I said, "art sure no
  Raven,
Ghastly, grim and long-tailed scullion, wand'ring from the kitchen
  floor—
Tell me what thy lordly will is, ere you leave my chamber door—"
    Quoth Ah Chung, "No shabby 'door.' " (*hic!*)

Much I marveled this ungainly brute to hear discourse so plainly,
Though his answer little meaning, little relevancy bore;
For we cannot help agreeing that no living human being
Ever yet was blest with seeing Chinaman outside his door
    With message like "*No shabby door.*"

Journalism wars among the various newspapers were as prevalent in
San Francisco as they had been in Nevada, and were riddled with an
equal—if not greater—amount of skulduggery. One especial thorn
in Twain's side, beginning when he was reporting from Nevada for
the *Call* and continuing during the time he lived and worked in San
Francisco, was Albert S. Evans. Evans, at first the San Francisco
correspondent for the Gold Hill *Evening News* of Washoe using the
pseudonym "Amigo," later became city editor of the San Francisco
Alta California, writing as "Fitz Smythe." He had served as the
Call's local reporter for several years prior to Twain's employment
there. The *Evening News* was in direct competition with the Virginia
City *Territorial Enterprise*, and the *Alta* competed with the *Call*, so in
a strictly professional sense there was no love lost between Twain
and Evans. But there was also an animosity between the two men
that went beyond the hollow staginess of trumped-up journalistic
feuds. Fitz Smythe hated anything that smacked of Bohemianism.
A rather petulant fellow who wore his morality on his bourgeois
sleeve, he staunchly championed the Protestant work ethic and
derided colorful journalistic artistes such as Twain, who often relied
more on flash than on serious research. Unfortunately for Evans, he
was no stylistic match for Twain. His writing, while voluminous,
was earnestly prosaic, clogged with malapropisms and infelicitous
turns of phrase. Hoping to savagely attack the Bohemian circle of

which Twain was part, Evans invented a pseudo-Bohemian character he called Armand Leonidas Stiggers, whom he claimed was his
"assistant" at the *Alta*. Stiggers had "weak blue eyes, delicate pink
hair" and "green spectacles" and he carried a "switch cane and
maroon-colored gloves." Accompanied by his vermin-infested
mutt Rienzi, Stiggers frequented Bohemian watering holes around
town where he ate and drank copiously, generally at the expense of
others. Evans used Stiggers as a foil in his *Alta* columns, but as a
parody of Bohemians he was a heavy-handed, limp-wristed caricature, and Twain lost no time in gleefully referring to *Evans* as
Stiggers. It is likely that Evans, once he began to be referred to
derisively as "Stiggers" by the San Francisco journalists, soon began to wish he had never dreamed up his mincing, improbable
assistant.

The rivalry between Twain and Fitz Smythe was fundamentally a
clash of progressive instincts with the status quo. Despite his muz-
zling by Barnes, Twain bristled with righteous indignation about
the corruption he saw daily in San Francisco's political institutions.
Evans, on the other hand, was frequently the mouthpiece for Chief
of Police Martin G. Burke as well as for other city officials. On the
surface, at least, Fitz Smythe's attacks tended to focus on what he
viewed as Twain's unsavory character, describing him as "the ab-
origine from the land of sage brush and alkali, whose soubriquet
was given him by his friends as indicative of his capacity for doing
the drinking for two." Evans would probably be nothing more than
a footnote in the history of San Francisco's frontier journalism had
he not coined the phrase which would designate Twain as the grand-
father of the Bohemian literary movement in California: he called
Twain the "Sagebrush Bohemian." For Fitz Smythe, those words
designated everything repugnant, barbaric, and incomprehensible.
In his horror, clumsily disguised as disgust, at Twain's freewheeling
spirit, Fitz Smythe can be viewed as the ancestor of all the literary
critics who would endlessly carp about Twain's personal peccadilloes in the hopes of diverting attention away from his basic
message.

*   *   *

The *Call* was clearly the wrong place for Twain to be plying his trade. George Barnes knew it, probably from the beginning; but he apparently said very little to his volatile lokulitems, preferring to let him reach the end of his rope by himself.

The turning point in Twain's tenure at the *Call* came when he was confronted head-on with the paper's ironclad policy of socio-political redlining. One day, while making his usual rounds, Twain observed a Chinese laundryman being pelted with stones by a group of young white bullies in full view of a local constable, who appeared to be enjoying the proceedings as much as the toughs. At the sight of this brutal tableau, Twain's lassitude instantly melted away and he dashed back to the *Call*, where he wrote up the incident with far more passion than he had felt for any story since going to work there. He duly submitted his article, in which he castigated the city of San Francisco for the racism of its police force, and went home satisfied that he had done a good turn for the oppressed Chinese population.

The next day he seized the paper as soon as it was printed and began scanning its columns for his item. To his disappointment and indignation, the article was nowhere to be seen.

Twain promptly marched up to the composing room, where he found the article in question "tucked away among condemned matter on the standing galley," as he later wrote. One of the printers told him that Barnes had been responsible for the exclusion of the item, so Twain went straight to his boss's office and demanded an explanation.

The eternally unflappable Barnes reminded his fiery reporter about the *Call*'s staunch supporters, the Irish working class. These people did not look kindly upon the new wave of Chinese immigrant labor that was sweeping into San Francisco, working for next to nothing and threatening to knock the Irish out of the labor market. If the *Call* suddenly took to publishing sentimental hogwash defending those coolies, said Barnes, then the paper's subscribers would most assuredly take their readership elsewhere.

Twain couldn't argue with the source of his paycheck, although the incident convinced him that his days at the *Call* were assuredly numbered. But the experience marked a turning point in his moral development. It set into motion in his mind a whole series of questions about the causes of man's inhumanity to man, questions for which he would not find hard answers until some years later. The Civil War, and the abolitionist position, had been uneasy matters for him. Likewise, when he had first seen the Indians of Nevada and California, he had reacted in a conventional, nineteenth-century manner, finding them uncouth and barbaric. But always he had felt the need to serve as the devil's advocate, teasing staunch Confederate ladies about a supposed "miscegenation society," and admitting that as debased as he believed the Paiute Indians to be, they should be pitied rather than scorned. As he matured, his moral sense would deepen until he could look back on the Civil War and write *Huckleberry Finn*, the greatest abolitionist novel of all, or compose an essay such as "Goldsmith's Friend Abroad Again," in which he would use the incident of the Chinese laundryman as a basis for a universal satire.

Despite the shakiness of his position at the *Call*, Twain remained optimistic about his Hale and Norcross stocks as a way out of scrivening servitude. Twain maintained in later years that he had purchased fifty shares on a margin by putting up twenty percent. The purchase had been a year earlier, when Hale and Norcross was booming at over a thousand dollars a share. By midsummer 1864, he was trembling on the edge of his seat as he waited for one last precipitous ascent so he could sell out and embark upon a life of ease and pleasure.

But, as he wrote in *Roughing It*, he waited too long.

> Something very important happened. The property holders of Nevada voted against the state constitution, but the folks who had nothing to lose were in the majority, and carried the measure over their heads. But after all it did not immediately look like a disaster, although unquestionably it was one. I hesitated, calculated the chances, and then concluded not to sell. Stocks went on rising; speculation went mad; bankers, merchants, lawyers, doctors, mechanics, laborers, even the very washerwomen and servant girls, were putting up their earnings on silver stocks, and every sun that rose in the

morning went down on paupers enriched and rich men beggared. What a gambling carnival it was! . . . And then, all of a sudden, out went the bottom and everything and everybody went to ruin and destruction! The wreck was complete. The bubble scarcely left a microscopic moisture behind it. I was an early beggar and a thorough one. My hoarded stocks were not worth the paper they were printed on. I threw them all away.

The heartsick would-be millionaire surveyed his suddenly unbearable situation, and was so distressed that he did the unthinkable—he stayed away from his desk at the *Call* for a day after the disaster, which worked a mighty hardship on that stream-lined paper. Twain returned to work the following day, resolving to "put up with my thirty-five dollars a week [actually it was forty] and forget all about it."

But the torpor he had been keeping at bay now suddenly roared in to engulf him like a vast, oily wave. He found his work so wearing that George Barnes began keeping an increasingly watchful eye on his fading lokulitems, and was seen to shake his head more and more at the sketchy quality of Twain's copy. Even the advent of a large earthquake that October failed to arouse Twain's interest. He managed to grind out a series of reports in which he focused on the human-interest angle of the event, but it was plain that his heart was not in his work.

With things so dismal in Twain's life, it was only a matter of time before Smiggy McGlural made his fateful entrance, bringing down the curtain on Twain's stint at the *Call*. Toward the end of his four months as lokulitems, Twain asked Barnes if his workload might not be cut back, along with his pay, which would be reduced from forty to twenty-five dollars a week. Barnes agreed, and suggested that Twain find himself an assistant to expedite his news gathering.

While he complained to Barnes about the long hours, Twain kept the real truth to himself—he wanted to quit the *Call*, but he couldn't afford to. His temperament was ill-suited to the exhausting, detail-oriented labors of local news-gathering, and his writing effectively censored by the *Call*'s adamant demographics. The reduced hour ploy was just a delaying tactic: Twain knew that the axe was due to fall, and in short order, too—but in the meanwhile he could use the money.

The origins of Smiggy McGlural are shrouded in mystery. Twain described him in his *Autobiography* as "a great hulking creature down in the counting room—good-natured, obliging, unintellectual—and he was getting little or nothing a week and boarding himself. A graceless boy of the counting-room force who had no reverence for anybody or anything was always making fun of this beachcomber, and he had a name for him which somehow seemed intensely apt and descriptive—I don't know why. He called him Smiggy McGlural."

It is probable that Twain had more than a hand in inventing this Frankenstein's monster of a novice lokulitems. A character called variously Smiggy McGuirrel or Maglooral appeared in several minstrel show songs of the era, as well as in humorous articles in the popular press. One of these articles, which ran in the *Golden Era* about this time, was called "Smiggy McGlural's Speech—A Bold Stroke for the Presidency," and described a fast-talking Irish demagogue's glib shot at the Oval Office. It is likely that Twain, as an avid fan of minstrel shows and a member of the local press, was familiar with the Smiggy character, and merely appropriated him for autobiographical effect many years later.

Impersonating this honey-tongued son of Erin, Twain sought out his victim—who has been identified as one William McGrew—and lay siege to him, persuading him that being the assistant of a lokulitems was a life unmatched in excitement and glory. McGrew/McGlural, needless to say, had no journalistic background, but as Twain observed in his *Autobiography*, "Mentality was not required or needed in a *Morning Call* reporter and so he conducted his office to perfection."

With commendable energy, McGlural leapt forth into the journalistic arena. As Twain played an ever-smaller role in the writing department, Smiggy's almost manic enthusiasm sometimes threatened to knock the *Call*'s stolid columns off their foundations. Here, for instance, is Smiggy's breezy description of a costume ball:

"Terpsichore and Apollo met at the Pavilion last night with their host of retainers. Orpheus was there with them; and with music and with dancing the hours wore away, until the time of night was represented by the small figures . . . Apollo, and old Charon himself, were industriously doing the agreeable. The affair passed off finely. There was no lack of enjoyment." Especially for Twain.

George Barnes was discreet, reserved, patient. But at last he summoned Twain to the inner sanctum. The accused shuffled in, aiming his gaze on the floor and scraping one foot after the other as he was wont to do when disaster loomed. Barnes fixed Twain with a knowing scowl and demanded point-blank, "Do you know what I think of you as a local reporter?"

Twain had to answer in the negative. He had some idea, it was true, but there was no need to hang himself prematurely.

"You're out of your element, Clemens. This position requires persistence and a certain attention to detail. I believe you are unsuited to it. Besides, you're obviously capable of greater things in literature."

"Oh, I see. You mean to say that I don't suit you," replied Twain with mock diffidence.

"Yes, to be truthful, that's exactly what I mean," admitted Barnes.

Twain was relieved to offer his resignation, even though it meant that he no longer had twenty-five dollars a week to squander on such luxuries as food and lodging. But he had to admit to himself that Barnes had been pretty slow; after all, he himself had known from his first agonizing morning at the *Call* that he was totally unfit for the toils of a lokulitems.

In 1906, when Mark Twain was finishing out his life as a nationally acclaimed man of letters—"a scribbler of books, and an immovable fixture among the other rocks of New England"—he had reason to remember his dismissal from the *Morning Call*. It was in April of that year that the famous San Francisco earthquake and fire drew international attention to the city by the bay, with lurid descriptions

screaming forth from the pages of every newspaper, and dramatic photos of the twisted, smoking wreckage.

By chance, one of the first photographs Twain saw happened to show the remains of the *Call* building, with the magnificent structure's ruined walls crumbling around its blackened foundation. (The *Call*, like Twain, had prospered in the intervening years, and had taken up far more palatial quarters as its fortunes grew.)

Twain was in the process of dictating notes for his *Autobiography* at the time of the earthquake, and as a result of seeing the picture of the ruined *Call* building he was moved to point out that even though Providence had been a little late in wreaking vengeance on the *Call* for firing him some forty years earlier, that vengeance had finally arrived. When providence finally decided to get down to business, said Twain, it had done an admirable job of it. He observed that it did seem a little extreme that Providence had chosen to reduce most of San Francisco to rubble in order to demolish the *Call* building, but to back up the judgment of the heavenly retribution committee he cited the case of a man who went home swearing from a prayer meeting. Nine months later, that man's wife and children all died long, agonizing deaths (shades of "The Massacre at Dutch Nick's"). It didn't really seem fair, Twain mused, but the ways of providence were often difficult to fathom. Providence had intended to punish the man for his blasphemy, and if the man had any intelligence, he probably realized that the intention had been carried out, although mainly at the expense of other people. But, reasoned Twain, *he* had known all along that sooner or later providence would even up the score with the *Call*—after all, he had been raised a Presbyterian, with an unshakable faith in the power of good over evil.

4

The Sagebrush Bohemian

The San Francisco of the mid-1860s was the child of Nevada's Comstock Lode, its lifeblood the streams of gold and silver that flowed from the mines and mills of the West. It was a boomtown with a thyroid problem, a punk kid rapidly growing too big for its britches. On its dank sand hills the flimsy wooden lean-tos of the 1850s were being displaced by the marble mausoleums of mineral monarchs, but many of the city's large downtown thoroughfares were paved with gap-toothed cobblestones or, more likely, wooden planks. Dirt streets were quite common throughout the sixties, until the advent of highly touted "Nicholson pavement"—wooden blocks on a base of asphalt or hard-packed sand.

The lawless fifties had seen vigilante gangs roaming the streets with blood in their collective eye, but as the Mother Lode waned and the Comstock Lode waxed, the vigilance committees were replaced by a more socially acceptable municipal government complete with police corruption. By the mid-sixties the city boasted all the trappings of civilization: schools, libraries, theatres, churches, a flourishing red light district—and the most vigorous Bohemian literary scene in the country.

San Francisco's first literary publication, begun in 1852 by J. M. Foard and Mark Twain's later *Enterprise* cohort Rollin M. Daggett, was the weekly *Golden Era*. At first the *Era* adhered to a homely format befitting its flannel-shirted, bewhiskered readership in California mining towns and settlements. Its four pages offered fiction and verse, news rewrites gleaned from other publications, various columns, and advertising. A "Correspondents' Column" grudgingly welcomed submissions by the great unwashed, which were published with often trenchant editorial commentary attached. Foard and Daggett evidently had their fingers on the public pulse, for a month after its inception the new publication boasted 2,000 circulation within the city of San Francisco, and it rapidly added another 1,100 paid subscribers in mining camps elsewhere in the state.

As San Francisco swelled from outpost to metropolis, the *Era* kept pace. By 1860 it had outlasted most of its more pretentious competitors in the literary field and was, in the words of contributor Charles Warren Stoddard, "the cradle and grave of many a high hope—there was nothing to be compared with it that side of the Mississippi." Fledgling writers inevitably made their first appearances in its six-column pages; bigger names, including John Phoenix, Alonzo "Old Block" Delano, and others, contributed with a little less frequency, as the *Era*'s pay scale of five dollars a column (for prose—poems were published as a favor to their authors) made scribbling for the *Era* a luxury rather than a livelihood.

In 1860 the *Era* changed hands, being sold by Foard and Daggett to "Colonel" Joseph Lawrence and James Brooks. Joe Lawrence seized the editorial reins, and the *Era* leaped gloriously forward into the annals of American literature.

Lawrence was smooth, urbane, and distinguished, and he sought contributors who would reflect the increasing sophistication of San Francisco itself. Like a literary spider he ensconced himself in the bar of the Lick House, and later at the Occidental Hotel, where he lured the cream of local writing talent for congenial imbibement and witty conversation. Then he set about fashioning new columns to describe the tone of life in the city.

He had as flamboyant a cast of characters to draw upon as ever were assembled in one place at one time. By the early sixties San Francisco had its share of transplanted New York Bohemians, an admittedly motley crew. The New Yorkers in turn had gathered at Pfaff's restaurant on Broadway, where they self-consciously imitated the "true" Bohemians of Paris and London while hobnobbing with their own celebrities such as Walt Whitman and William Dean Howells. Although the crew from Pfaff's had varying effects on the California literary scene, California, for its part, had made quite an impact on these East Coast refugees, for its frontier atmosphere was more conducive to originality, even inconoclasm. The European-style Bohemianism that was flourishing in New York had, by the late 1850s, become too intent on hero worship, making the Bohemian scene in New York almost a caricature of Parisian Bohemianism, with all its tubercular existentialism and wretched excess. In San Francisco this hothouse quality rapidly evaporated when it was exposed to the homespun, no-nonsense attitudes of the booming pioneer city. The coming together of the seemingly disparate elements of European intellectualism and Pacific coast empiricism ultimately created one of history's most exciting intellectual atmospheres. (That hybrid, incidentally, was so vigorous that it has survived in some measure until the present day, as evidenced by the beat and hippie movements of the 1950s and 1960s.) With the advantage of hindsight, most historians of the California Bohemian movement list Mark Twain as the major talent of the milieu.

The literary San Francisco with which Mark Twain would become embroiled contained more colorful characters per square foot than anywhere else on earth. The *Golden Era* under Joe Lawrence published them all. There was Prentice Mulford, for instance, known to his *Era* readers as "Dogberry"—a cheerfully poverty-stricken recluse who lived on a decrepit houseboat and wrote variously about mining, spiritualism, and the arts. Mulford was so shy and retiring that he sometimes waited for hours in the street near the *Era*'s office, manuscript in hand, before he could get up the courage to walk in, even though he was one of the paper's most popular contributors.

There was Joaquin Miller, a bearded poseur fresh from the wilds of Oregon, with his charming wife Minnie Myrtle. Miller's literary beginnings in California were quite inauspicious—when Joe Lawrence looked over some of Miller's fledgling odes to the glories of Nature, he had observed that Miller should abandon versifying forthwith and return to Oregon to "grow taters." Miller persisted, however, and eventually became a patron saint of Bohemia in northern California after making a big splash in Europe. Miller's poetry is hardly considered fashionable today, but he left something of a legacy by serving in his old age as a mentor to second-generation Bohemian George Sterling, who in turn influenced Jack London.

There was Adah Isaacs Menken, a voluptuous *femme fatale* whose histrionics predated those of future daughters of public tragedy such as Isadora Duncan. Menken considered herself a poet, but her main claim to fame was as the chief attraction of a sensationalistic play called *Mazeppa*, during which she galloped across the stage tied to the back of a stallion, clad only in a skimpy undergarment. Of her attempts at poetry, a single opening line should suffice: "Years and years the songless soul waited to drift out beyond the sea of pain where the shapeless life was wrecked."

Then there was Ina Coolbrith, eventually California's first poet laureate, a young and lovely woman with a tragic and secret past involving Mormonism (her uncle was Joseph Smith, the Church of the Latter-day Saints' charismatic leader) and a marriage to a brutal drunkard in the pueblo of Los Angeles, which she had fled to San Francisco to escape. Coolbrith wrote a great deal of poetry, but she earned a living as a librarian in Oakland and San Francisco, encouraging many young writers. Coolbrith and Menken would both become close, in different ways, to Mark Twain.

And there was Francis Bret Harte, who was a quarter Jewish and a native of upstate New York. Harte had emigrated to San Francisco as a boy in the mid-fifties with his family. In 1857 he drifted up to Humboldt County in northern California to visit his sister Margaret, and there he remained for three years, clerking in a drugstore and working sporadically as a teacher. Eventually, being of a bookish nature, he acquired the trade of typesetting at the Uniontown

Northern Californian, going on to become a very acceptable assistant editor. He was serving as editor-in-chief during the absence of the paper's publisher when an incident occurred that altered the course of Harte's life. The settlers of Humboldt County had been waging a bitter war against the local Indian tribes, and during Harte's editorship of the *Northern Californian* a group of enraged whites captured an island encampment of Indians opposite the town of Eureka. Although the tribe was a peaceable one, the attackers mounted a brutal offensive during which dozens of Indian men, women, and children were slaughtered. Harte, backed by many voices of conscience in the community, lashed out with a furious editorial, which so enraged the perpetrators and other rough elements that Harte had no choice but to flee back to San Francisco and civilization.

There he obtained work as a compositor at the *Golden Era*, which also published his short stories and verse. His studious and modest mien, coupled with his steadily growing ability as a writer, won him powerful friends in San Francisco. Jessie Benton Fremont, wife of General John Fremont, took him under her matronly wing and encouraged him to continue the pursuit of literature. Thomas Starr King, the Unitarian clergyman and eloquent spokesman for the Union, enlisted Harte's aid in composing stirring lyrics for the Northern cause. In exchange, King introduced Harte to Robert B. Swain, the superintendent of the United States Mint. Swain gave Harte what was in effect a sinecure—a position as his private secretary, with the lightest of workloads and a handsome salary of two hundred dollars a month. There was a tacit understanding that Harte would use the time to hone his literary craft, and that was just what he did. Many of his fellow scribblers, who had to fight tooth and nail for survival, resented Harte's comfort, ease, and influential allies. He was not an altogether popular figure in San Francisco literary circles. Charles Webb, one of Harte's closest friends and his fellow *Era* contributor, described him as a person who "occupies a highly responsible and lucrative position in the Mint—with very little to do." The more rakish Bohemians also sneered at Harte's domestic life. At the time of his ascension to the U.S. Mint, Harte had just recently married Anna Griswold, a contralto in the choir of

Starr King's church. Instead of spending long hours discussing the meaning of life and art in Barbary Coast taverns, the mild-mannered Harte was more likely to be found fooling with wallpaper paste or pruning shears around his Oakland cottage. The wags and wits of the literary underclass were fond of asking the not entirely rhetorical question, "How can a suburban drone write a column called 'The Bohemian Feuilleton?' "

Mark Twain had met Bret Harte when both men were working in the same three-story brick building on Commercial Street—Harte in the sumptuous third-floor offices of the U.S. Mint annex, and Twain down below in the more mundane headquarters of the *Morning Call*. The main branch of the Mint was housed in a large and imposing structure at Fifth and Mission streets, but those quarters had grown so crowded during the city's recent flush period that a number of its most important employees had been literally squeezed out. The superintendent and his secretary had thus been obliged to remove to the building where the miserable Twain's career as a lokulitems was lapsing into its tragicomic diminuendo.

It was in the Mint annex that Twain and Harte became friends, of sorts. The two men were about the same age—both in their late twenties—but there all similarity ended. Harte was reserved, fastidious; he was such a perfectionist in his work that he had been known to fill a wastebasket with rough drafts of an acceptance to a social invitation. He dressed foppishly, his hallmark being an exquisite little necktie of brilliant hue. That necktie irritated Twain so much that he mentioned it in his autobiography forty years later. "Always it was of a single color, and intense," he sneered. "Most frequently, perhaps, it was crimson—a flash of flame under his chin; or it was indigo blue and as hot and vivid as if one of those splendid and luminous Brazilian butterflies had lighted there."

Twain, on the other hand, embodied the snide sobriquet bestowed on him by Fitz Smythe—he was called "the Bohemian from the sage-brush," and with his disheveled attire, defiant slouch, and drawling sarcasm he was a virtual antithesis to Harte's epigrammatic dandyism. But despite the fact that Twain was a Bohemian who wasn't so sure he wanted to be one, while Harte called himself a

Bohemian but was actually a suburbanite, the two young men struck up a friendship that was to last a number of years.

At the time Twain met Harte, Twain had been published several times in the *Golden Era*. His contributions were articles about his previous visits to San Francisco while he was still on the staff of the *Enterprise*. Now, having served his apprenticeship as a newspaper reporter, Twain felt that it was high time he advanced beyond political reporting and oddball observations on civic events—even though those were often his strongest subjects—and struck out for more literary territory. He found a navigator in Bret Harte, who with Charles Webb had founded a literary weekly called the *Californian* just a few months earlier.

It was only logical that sooner or later that hallmark of civilization, the literary magazine, would rear its head in San Francisco. Twain himself observed in *Roughing It* that the appearance of such publications indicated beyond question that a Western city had "arrived." "[T]here is one other sign [of] prosperity; it comes last, but when it does come it establishes beyond cavil that the 'flush times' are at the flood. This is the birth of the 'literary' paper."

Harte and Webb, chafing under the mining-camp provincialism of the crude old *Era*, had in fact begun joking about the new magazine in their *Era* columns several months before the *Californian* made its entrance. Webb, whose pseudonym was "Inigo," suggested that the new journal be called *Inigo's Weekly Watchman*. Harte proposed that the forthcoming periodical should be published entirely in French in order to show just how sophisticated and "literary" San Francisco had become. Webb made fun of Harte's morals, insinuating that since Harte was, after all, a married man, he should only be allowed to deal with the more homely of the magazine's future contributors. (This was one comment on Harte's distinctly non-Bohemian private life; in another of his columns Webb had mockingly expressed concern over the fact that although the *Era's* contributors were all staid and respectable citizens, he was concerned about Bret's drinking and loose living.)

The *Californian* premiered in May 1864, just as Twain was beginning his toil for the *Call*. Webb served as chief editor, and Harte was its primary contributor. In the Mint annex he spent many a publicly funded hour turning out articles and columns for the new publication. Whenever Twain happened to step into Harte's office to pass the time of day, he found Harte studying over well-turned phrases, and he was duly impressed.

Harte soon persuaded Twain to shift his allegiance from the *Era* to the *Californian*. Just as he had been eager in Virginia City to join the hard-drinking, hoax-loving brotherhood of frontier journalists on the *Enterprise*, Twain was now anxious to find acceptance as a full-fledged member of the San Francisco literati. Twain felt keenly the stigma of being an itinerant reporter from the wilds of Washoe. There was a part of him that reveled in his reputation as "the Wild Humorist of the Pacific Slope"—a reputation he had studiously cultivated in Nevada—but he was distinctly uncomfortable with the less savory connotations that went with this image. From the moment he took up residence in San Francisco, he had sought out the company of clergymen, important government figures, and other respectable citizens as a counterbalance to the company he kept in his lodging houses, at the city jail, or on the Barbary Coast.

Therefore, when Harte began to eloquently limn the praises of the *Californian*, Twain was quick to see the advantage of appearing in its pages. Whereas the *Era* was a paper with a distinctly regional outlook, the aura surrounding the *Californian* was cosmopolitan to a fault. Twain was soon writing to his mother and sister, "I quit the *Era*, long ago. It wasn't high-toned enough. The *Californian* circulates among the highest class of the community, and it is the best weekly literary paper in the United States."

His contributions show that he was beginning to acquire a jocular, loose-jointed style of writing, a style he would refine but never completely abandon. In one of his weekly articles, he grumbled at great length about the discomfort of driving out to the Cliff House early in the morning. He admitted, however, to enjoying the view—filtered through the bottom of a whiskey glass. In another piece he announced, "Some people are not particular about what sort of company they keep. Now for several days I have been visiting the Board of Brokers, and associating with brokers, and drinking with them, and swapping lies with them, and being as familiar and sociable with them as I would with the most respectable people in the world." He then went on to describe the stockbrokers' peculiar lingo and some of the other goings-on at the Hall of the San Francisco Board of Brokers—better known, as he pointed out, as the "Den of the Forty Thieves."

This sort of article, along with the blistering attacks on the San Francisco Police Department he was writing for the *Enterprise*, seem to indicate that Twain's thinking was gradually progressing from burlesque humor to (attempted) moralizing and philosophy. Much to the amusement of the sophisticated Harte and Webb, Twain appeared feverishly anxious to shake the alkali dust from his shoes and banish the specter of "frontier humorist" from his writing image—even if it was to his own detriment. The hand of Webb was evident in one of a series of letters in which various *Californian* contributors ostensibly submitted their applications for the paper's editorship, and specified what changes they would make. This letter, supposedly written by Twain, was the funniest of the bunch. It was signed, "Yours 'Mark Twain Surnamed the Moral Phenomenon,' " and, poking fun at Twain's Presbyterian upbringing, it chastised the paper for supplying its readers with "too much wicked wit and too much demoralizing humor. . . . What the people are suffering for is Morality," trumpeted "Twain." "Turn them over to me . . . I can fetch them!"

The *Californian* served as a springboard for California writers, publishing the restrained but evocative verse of Ina Coolbrith, the quirky humor of Prentice Mulford, and the dry and killing wit of Ambrose Bierce. The politesse of Harte was evident in the paper's disdain for "local color" and the myth of the "honest miner" and the "noble pioneer." Harte enquired "whether the individual who contributed a fund of impious slang to the national vocabulary was peculiarly estimable as a moral teacher." No doubt shuddering as he recalled his narrow escape from the backwoods, he savaged the picturesque place names so dear to the hearts of California regionalists, dismissing colorful designations like Whiskey Diggins and Poker Flat as "outright offences against public decency." Going a step farther, Harte used the pages of the *Californian* to express derision at the pioneer ethic of hard work and faith; the *Californian's* existentialist *littérateur* went so far as to suggest that hard work and faith were their own punishment rather than their own reward.

Despite the fact that the *Californian* was well received all over the Pacific Coast and even made a few waves back in civilization (New York), it was undoubtedly too far ahead of its time to secure a large pool of paying readers and advertisers, and as a result it suffered from the severe financial irregularities that literary journals inevitably seem to encounter. The paper remained under the financial proprietorship of Charles Webb for only a few months; when funding grew dubious, Webb was forced to sell out to a group of printers to whom he owed money, although he continued to edit the paper. Harte remained as a steady contributor and major influence on the paper throughout its existence, and served as editor in Webb's absences.

The *Californian* survived only four years before it folded. Long after it was just a memory of the awakening of literature in San Francisco, Webb recalled, "The *Californian* nearly bankrupted me in an inconceivably short time." But the paper had served its purpose. It had begun the conversion of "the Wild Humorist of the Pacific Slope" into the "Moral Phenomenon," and, along with the literary developments it represented, it had been for Mark Twain a guiding light along the path of literary rectitude.

5

Sex and Suicide: The Secret Life of Samuel Clemens

After he lost his position on the *Morning Call*, Twain, now minus his weekly paycheck, was obliged to depend on the income he received from contributing to various publications. The financially erratic life seems to have struck a chord of discomfort in the mind of our ex–future millionaire, for, as he wrote in *Roughing It*, "I became a very adept at slinking. I slunk from back street to back street, I slunk away from approaching faces that looked familiar, I slunk to my meals, ate them humbly and with mute apology for every mouthful I robbed my generous landlady of, and at midnight, after wanderings that were but slinkings away from cheerfulness and light, I slunk to my bed."

Most likely these slinkings were literary rather than literal, for even before leaving the *Call*'s employ Twain had worked out a deal with his former *Enterprise* boss, Joe Goodman, to write a daily article for that paper, the only stipulation being that the submission should deal with life in San Francisco. The pay for these articles was to be thirty dollars a week. Twain also reviewed plays for the *Dramatic Chronicle*, which was paying him forty dollars a month for his services. These sums may not have been princely, but presumably they were sufficient to prevent Twain from abject slinkage.

If Twain did indeed have misgivings about his livelihood, they may have sprung from the fear of financial failure that dogged him throughout his life. As a child, he had witnessed the struggle of his father, John Marshall Clemens, to support the Clemens family—a task at which the elder Clemens had not been particularly adept. Bad judgment had prompted Twain's father to make various ill-advised business investments, ending when he cosigned on a note for a man who subsequently refused to pay the debt. Despite his lack of financial wherewithal, John Clemens paid off the defaulted loan, losing everything he had in the process. His son Samuel, still in his teens, had been forced out into the world to become a printer's apprentice, and never really returned home again. (Ironically, at the time of his death a few years later, John Clemens had finally secured a lucrative appointment as a county justice of the peace, but while returning from the county seat after being sworn in, he caught a severe chill from riding horseback in the cold weather, and the resulting pneumonia killed him.)

The Clemens and Lampton families from whom Samuel Clemens was descended were Southern gentry, proud of their aristocratic British forebears but mired in a mundane present of shabby gentility. From an early age, Samuel recognized the presence of class divisions in society, and deeply felt the ignominy of coming from a "good" family that nonetheless had no real security in life, moving from place to place in search of opportunities that never quite materialized. For the rest of his life Clemens would be feverishly keen on instant-wealth schemes, from mining speculation to inventions and patents. His most deeply rooted fear was financial ruin, and he would not be able to shake it even after, some years later, his personal worth grew to over a million dollars.

To add to his discomfort, his departure from the *Call*, as logical as it was, had been duly noted and commented upon by numerous cynical scribes around town, and the criticism rankled. Fitz Smythe, for whom the opportunity was heaven sent, crowed that Clemens "says he left the *Call* because 'They wanted me to w-o-r-k a-t n-i-g-h-t-s, and d-a-m-n m-e if I'll work n-i-g-h-t-s for any man a l-i-v-i-n-g!" With such commentary in the municipal press, word rapidly got around San Francisco that the "Sagebrush Bohemian" had become a wandering prodigal. The worst of it was that the change in Twain's circumstances was duly noted by the wealthy, influential people he had been carefully cultivating. One of these was Captain Edward Poole, whose wife, passing the intersection of Clay and Montgomery streets one day, espied the late lokulitems lounging beneath a lamppost with a cigar box tucked beneath his arm. Twain had been an occasional dinner guest in the Poole home, and therefore Mrs. Poole, who had a reputation as a wit, extended her hand and greeted him: "Why, Mark, where are you going in such a hurry?"

"I'm m-o-o-v-i-n-g," Twain drawled, raising the lid of the box to reveal a pair of soiled socks, a pipe, and two paper shirt collars.

In a letter to Orion and Mollie Clemens written during this period, Twain admitted that he was in debt. "But," he added, "I have gone to work in dead earnest to get out. Joe Goodman pays me $100 a month for a daily letter, and the Dramatic Chronicle pays me $—or rather *will* begin to pay me, next week—$40 a month for dramatic criticisms . . . You are in trouble, & in debt—" he continued, in answer to a letter which he had just received from his brother, in which Orion was apparently complaining about the recent loss of his territorial secretaryship and the hardships he was facing, "so am I. I am utterly miserable—so are you. Perhaps your religion will sustain you, will feed you—I place no dependence in mine. Our religions are alike, though, in one respect—neither can make a man happy when he is out of luck. If I do not get out of debt in 3 months—pistols or poison for one—exit *me*."

Apparently Twain meant business about the "pistols or poison," for many years later he wrote in the margin of his copy of the *Letters of James Russell Lowell* about an "experience of 1866 [*sic*] when I put the pistol to my head but wasn't man enough to pull the trigger. Many times I have been sorry I did not succeed, but I was never ashamed of having tried. Suicide is the only really sane thing the young or the old ever do in this life."

Twain's impecunious circumstances had a number of far-reaching consequences. Not the least of these was that his precarious financial state effectively prevented him from assuming matrimonial ties. Romance was no stranger to our red-headed hero, although he managed to keep his private life most strictly private—not an easy feat in the roisterous atmosphere of Virginia City or San Francisco, and even more difficult considering the fact that Twain was in both cities the most public of public figures.

In Virginia City his exploits had often been the fodder for sniping by rival journalists. Twain's frequent appearances at Odd Fellows' and firemen's dances—where the few "decent" women of marriageable age in the district went to discreetly showcase their availability—led to numerous squibs in the Virginia City *Union*, the Gold Hill *Daily News*, and other sheets, accusing the *Enterprise*'s dashing reporter of numerous affairs of the heart. In one such article, the local of the Gold Hill *Daily News*, having trudged the four miles uphill to Virginia City in search of grist for the mill, was seized by a bout of sentiment as he observed schoolchildren at play. The sight of those innocents, he declared, put him in memory of the time "when we made dirt pies, spun tops, and played 'keep house' with the little girls. But now we are a man; like Mark Twain, we can't find nary a one to keep house with. Mark says he 'popped it' to one the other day, but she couldn't see it. Guess we won't try it."

Tom Fitch, editor of the *Daily Union* and a neighbor of Twain and Dan De Quille in Virginia City, was fond of retelling a story about Twain's romantic reputation. It seems that during the Christmas season of 1863, Fitch and Rollin Daggett of the *Enterprise* were sitting in the smoking room of their hotel, waiting for dinner, when a messenger boy arrived and dropped off a parcel addressed to Samuel Clemens. Said Fitch:

> After his departure we examined the bundle, for we were communists in spirit, and found that it contained a pretty knitted woolen scarf and a card bearing the inscription, "Mr. Samuel L. Clemens, from his friend Etta." "I can improve on that message," suggested Daggett, who was the wag and philosophical disputant and cribbage player of the club, and, obtaining a sheet of note paper, he wrote in a fine female hand the following note:
> "Mr. Clemens: The accompanying scarf having been prepared as a Christmas gift to you, it has been determined not to divert it from its

original destination, although a knowledge of your late conduct having come to the ears of the writer your own conscience will tell you that this must close all communication between us, in which decision my father and mother concur. Your former friend, Etta."

The scarf was rewrapped and with this note tied to it was placed in Sam's room. Shortly afterward he made his appearance and proceeded to his room to prepare for dinner. Soon we heard the crockery going. "What is the matter, Sam?" said Daggett. Thereupon entered Mark Twain, with the coat and collar off, and throwing the package upon the table, burst forth: "Read that. That's just my infernal luck. You hounds can run the town night after night and nobody ever says a word, but I am found out at once."

Nothing more is known of "Etta" or her relationship with Twain; perhaps she was the young lady who ostensibly refused to enter into conjugal bliss with him. Joe Goodman mentioned a romance gone sour in an editorial announcing Twain's departure for San Francisco in the wake of the Sanitary Fund fracas. Explaining that Twain's departure was at least partly a flight from a slighted lover, Goodman went on to ponder, "Who ever thought beneath that ingenuous face was concealed a heart that could wrong confiding innocence? Yet the angels fell, and why not Mark Twain?" He affixed the following verses:

——to Mark Twain

At morn, at noon, in evening light
As in a dream I move around,
For Heaven has lost its loveliest sight
And earth its sweetest sound.
Do fond emotions softly swell
For her from whom your steps have strayed
Or has some flaunting city belle
Eclipsed your plighted sage-brush maid?
Mark Twain, Mark Twain,
Ah, haste again
To her whose true love you betrayed.

Twain himself had absolutely nothing to say on the subject of his romantic life. When the odious Fitz Smythe in San Francisco intimated that the *Call*'s lokulitems was frequenting "love stores" on the Barbary Coast, had lost his watch to a strumpet, and had ostensibly picked up a "social disease," Twain did not respond—whether from outraged dignity or tacit acquiescence we don't know. But in his Western writing he often gave himself away, as in a description of a seance presided over by a Mrs. Foye, "a good-looking, earnest-faced, pale-red-haired, neatly dressed, young woman standing on a little stage behind a small deal table with slender legs and no drawers—the table, understand me; I am writing in a hurry."

In another piece, written in San Francisco for the *Enterprise*, he described women's fashions, apparently one of his pet subjects, for he returned to it more than once. Describing the then-current style of hoop skirts, he observed, "To critically examine these hoops—to get the best effect—one should stand on the corner of Montgomery and look up a steep street like Clay or Washington. As the ladies loop their dresses up until they lie in folds and festoons on the spreading hoop, the effect presented by a furtive glance up a steep street is very charming. It reminds me of how I used to peep under circus tents when I was a boy and see a lot of mysterious legs tripping about with no visible bodies attached to them. And what handsome vari-colored, gold-clasped garters they wear now-a-days!"

In a letter written to Orion's wife Mollie from Aurora early in 1862, he had presented his rationale for not marrying. "I am not married yet, and I never *will* marry until I can afford to have servants enough to leave my wife in the position for which I designed her, viz: as a companion. I don't want to sleep with a three-fold Being who is cook, chambermaid and washerwoman all in one. I don't mind sleeping with female servants as long as I am a bachelor—by *no means*—but after I marry, that sort will be 'played out' you know." Couched in terms that were obviously designed for shock value (Mollie Clemens was a pillar of propriety, and her brother-in-law loved nothing more than baiting pious moralists),

Twain's agenda was nonetheless clear enough: Until he had the wherewithal to move in social circles where the women fit his notion of acceptability, he would remain single. In the meanwhile, being a young and gregarious male with normal appetites, and living in a frontier society with few of the strictures of the more settled East, his private life was not likely to be monastic, whatever he purveyed as the "official story."

In later years, he claimed that he had only been truly in love once in his life, with a fourteen-year-old girl named Laura Wright whom he had met during his Mississippi piloting days. He had only known her for a few days, and then circumstances had sent him off in the opposite direction on his steamboat. They had agreed to write each other, but his letters were apparently intercepted by her parents, and the budding romance faltered and died. Twain recounted the poignant tale in his *Autobiography* many years later. Laura, he said, viewing her through the rosy mist of decades-old reminiscence, was "a frank and simple and winsome child who had never been away from home in her life before, and had brought with

THE GRACE OF A KANGAROO.

her to these distant regions the freshness and the fragrance of her own prairies." It made a wonderfully melancholy story: the pure, unspoiled backwoods girl, barely an adolescent; the "shipboard" romance; the meddling parents; the blighted hopes. For Twain, fact and fiction were often inextricable. But his life in San Francisco was far from what he had known in Missouri, and the women he knew in the West were far more complex than Laura Wright, real or imagined, had been.

Two women whose social and class status made Twain consider them unsuitable as marriage material nonetheless attracted his attention during this period. Of one relationship, only contradictory stories exist. Regarding the other, it seems that there was mutual interest, as well as rivalry for the woman in question. These were certainly not the only affairs or attractions Twain experienced during this period of his life. But since the women involved were public figures, in their cases the curtain of obscurity which tends to shroud Twain's private life parts slightly to reveal intriguing hints and glimpses, if no definite answers.

Of the two women, Ina Coolbrith was closer to what Twain might have viewed as marriage material, but ultimately, there were simply too many obstacles. Coolbrith was no more than twenty-two when she first met Mark Twain in the offices of San Francisco's *Golden Era*, for which she wrote poetry under the *noms de plume* of "Ina" and "Meg Merrilies." A tall, slender, strikingly beautiful young woman with masses of dark curly hair and luminous, deep-set eyes, Coolbrith exuded an air of reticent tragedy untainted by fashionable histrionics. Few among even her closest friends were aware that she was the niece of the Latter-day Saints' self-styled prophet Joseph Smith, and that she had experienced a tortuous childhood as her family had been driven, with the sect of Mormons, from one hostile state to another. Her father had died when she was very young; her mother remarried, and the family finally settled in the town of Los Angeles, some five hundred miles south of San Francisco. There Josephine Smith (she wouldn't change her name until she left Los Angeles several years later) attended grammar school in the dusty village of five thousand souls and grew to be the belle of the pueblo, leading the dancers at a grand ball on the arm of Don Pio Pico, the last Mexican governor of California.

She began writing poetry during this time, and when it was not only published in the Los Angeles *Star*, but also reprinted in San Francisco papers, she felt that she had found her career. But her marriage to Robert Carsley, owner of the Salamander Iron Works and player in a traveling minstrel group, ended her felicity. Carsley was given to bouts of drinking and fits of violent temper, and although his wife gave him no cause for jealousy, one day he returned from an out-of-town performing engagement and attacked her with scissors and a kitchen knife, accusing her of having had affairs with every man in town. He was restrained by Coolbrith's mother, and stormed off, only to return the next day with a six-shooter. The pueblo militia was hastily summoned when he began firing at his wife. Ina's stepfather, meanwhile, pulled his own weapon and shot at Carsley, and Carsley returned fire, wounding the older man in the hand, which later had to be amputated.

This was in December of 1861, a year when the pueblo was inundated with heavy rains. Ina obtained a divorce from Carsley, but faced with social ostracism, she chose to leave Los Angeles and the scene of her misery behind. Some months before the violent attack she had apparently borne Carsley a son who had died shortly thereafter; the anguish was altogether too painful, and she decided to try San Francisco, "city of mists and of dreams!" as she was to describe it in a poem many years later. Symbolically, she chose to leave her old name behind as well, adopting instead Ina (short for Josephine) Coolbrith (her mother's maiden name), and shaking off the ignominy of the surname Smith with all its Mormon associations.

Her family moved with her, and they settled down to life in the city by the bay, supported by Ina, who became an English teacher. Despite her family responsibilities, she turned out a steady stream of poetry, much of it painted in dark or steamy hues, recalling her blighted past in Los Angeles. It was received favorably by the

Golden Era and published frequently, and Ina became a member of San Francisco's Bohemian literary circle, along with Charles Webb, Charles Warren Stoddard, Bret Harte, and Mark Twain.

Stoddard, Harte, and Twain were her three favorites among the Bohemian males. Stoddard, an impetuous, emotionally volatile lad, worshipped Ina as a Muse between his sudden trips across the Pacific to the Sandwich Islands (later renamed the Hawaiian Islands) and Tahiti. He adored Coolbrith, but always from a distance. (He and Twain would remain friends, and when Twain roamed the world as a public lecturer some years later, he would hire Stoddard in London to accompany him, ostensibly as his "secretary," but actually as a companion.)

The distance between Harte and Coolbrith was more formally imposed; he was inextricably bound in the shackles of matrimony, although this apparently did not stop him from appreciating Coolbrith's beauty and intelligence. Harte was a frequent visitor to the Russian Hill home she shared with her family, and he remained the soul of propriety as he sat in the parlor with Ina discussing literature and philosophy, or in lighter moods inventing implausible limericks. Harte's appreciation of Ina seemed to be based on the realization that she was the embodiment of everything that Anna Griswold Harte lacked—intellect, a keen sensitivity to literature and the creative life, and physical attractiveness. Ina rarely mentioned Mrs. Harte, having once coolly observed that she was talented and witty, but not beautiful.

Coolbrith's experience with Robert Carsley had scarred her emotionally, leaving her timid and fearful about surrendering herself to another relationship. Nonetheless, her passionate, outgoing nature would not let her adopt the role of a bloodless old maid, or of a purely mental companion. She was drawn to Bret Harte, whom she always called Frank, and although he was out of reach physically, she enjoyed their platonic friendship; it supplied much of what she craved emotionally without threatening to degenerate into the physical danger and emotional pain of her doomed alliance with Carsley.

Mark Twain was something of an intruder into the relationship between Harte and Ina, and by all accounts Harte did not appreciate the competition. His relationship with Twain was already complex, with their respective personal and literary insecurities hopelessly tangled. Harte respected Twain's writing, but primarily as a diamond in the rough, while Twain found more to praise in Harte's literature than in his character, and sometimes wasn't even sure about the literature. Neither man was entirely comfortable with the other; each knew that the other had talent, even genius, but both were mutually reluctant to extend the appreciation to heartfelt personal friendship.

So when Twain began to appear in Ina's parlor, a guest along with Charlie Stoddard and Harte, Harte was resentful. The wags of Virginia and San Francisco were fond of teasing "the Bohemian from the sage-brush" about all the hearts he had supposedly broken; what if this redheaded savage broke poor Ina's heart? Harte felt a certain proprietary impulse toward Ina, telling himself that he wanted to guide her development as a writer; but the likelier case was that he was in love with her. Either way, the blustery entrance of Twain, like the proverbial bull in the china shop, did not please him.

Ina remained even-handed in her treatment of the two rivals, although she admitted privately that she found Twain handsome. Twain, as was his tendency, kept things light and breezy, exuding sociable charm, even flirting a bit, but refusing to be pinned down. Meanwhile he was probably engaging in his usual activity of objectively summing up the potential marriage partner. Unfortunately Ina presented some difficulties. He had met her family, they were far from well-to-do, and they did not move in the social circles he desired to enter. Ina herself had to work to support them, which, if he were completely honest with himself, he found slightly distasteful, being burdened by the notion of Southern chivalry that was the ironic legacy of his father. True, Ina was one of the prettiest girls on the Pacific coast, but he was always able to restrain his emotions in the service of sensible thinking. Moreover, he had heard rumors— which his own highly developed experience as a student of human foibles told him were probably valid—that Miss Coolbrith had a soiled past: a *mésalliance* in a frontier settlement, some skeleton in the family closet, perhaps. These things worked against her as marriage material. Her connection to Joseph Smith and the Mormons wasn't generally known, but Twain may have heard about it, even if only in the form of hearsay. In mid–nineteenth-century America, Latter-Day Saints were definitely beyond the pale socially. Twain's visit to Salt Lake City, the Mormons' headquarters, during his trip west in 1861, had left him with many vivid memories of the Latter-Day Saints and their leader, Brigham Young. Judging by his subsequent writing on the subject in *Roughing It* and elsewhere, the polygamous Mormons both intrigued and horrified him. Coolbrith herself was obviously aware of the social stigma attached to Mormonism, for she changed her name and attempted to alter her past history in order to purge it. Nonetheless, Samuel Clemens would never have married a Mormon, even if, like Ina, she were only a former Latter-Day Saint, fallen from grace in the eyes of the sect.

However, San Francisco's Bohemian gossips were soon buzzing over a heated exchange that had transpired between Twain and Bret Harte over Ina. The facts in the stories varied, but the substance remained the same: Twain, in a fit of fury, had called Harte a vile name and had accused him of pressing an unfair advantage with Coolbrith. Harte had responded with calculated coolness, but he was reported to be livid with rage. The disagreement was to have lingering effects, for it marked the beginning of the antagonism that would characterize the Twain/Harte relationship for the next several decades. It was a turning point; although neither rival would win Ina, their association with one another would never be quite the same.

After Twain and Harte had left San Francisco to seek their subsequent fortunes in the East—Twain to marry Olivia Langdon in 1870 and Harte to abandon and then divorce Anna Harte a number of years later—Ina Coolbrith, who remained single for the rest of her long life, went on to distinguish herself as a poet. She was widely published in Pacific coast journals, and near the end of her life was named California's poet laureate. As city librarian of Oakland in the 1880s she was a vital influence on a ragged young boy named Jack London, whom she introduced to the world of books and ideas. London would return the favor by writing glowingly of her in his novel *Martin Eden*. During the 1906 San Francisco earthquake and fire, the only manuscript of her memoirs was destroyed—a minor tragedy when compared with the wholesale destruction of that lusty city, perhaps, but a grave loss to the annals of California literature.

In retrospect, Ina Coolbrith and Mark Twain had some striking similarities: both were from the Midwest, and both had fled to San Francisco to escape something (in Coolbrith's case, her marriage and the stigma of Mormonism; in Twain's, the Civil War and the Sanitary Fund fiasco); both had adopted *noms de guerre* to obscure their pasts, and in doing so had inadvertently revealed more than they hid. But Coolbrith was to remain a Californian; she accepted the identity of her adopted state, and was a key figure in the California Bohemian movement. Twain, on the other hand, soaked up as much of California's Bohemian atmosphere as he could, and then moved on to the East Coast, where he would spend the rest of his life digesting his California experiences, and changing the face of American literature while mining his experiences for "pay dirt." Like Jack London, he owed Ina Coolbrith a debt, but unlike London, he never mentioned Coolbrith's name anywhere in his writings. The fact is probably significant.

A "horse" of an altogether different color was Adah Isaacs Menken, who blew into San Francisco in February of 1863 and took that boisterous town by storm as the chief attraction in a rather hackneyed play called *Mazeppa*. Menken played the male lead, and at the climactic moment she was stripped before the gaping audience at Maguire's Opera House, retaining nothing but a flesh-colored body stocking. Thereupon she was strapped to the back of a fiery black stallion, which raced wildly up an imaginary mountain while the audience sat transfixed.

These theatrical excesses were viewed and reviewed by Mark Twain, who sent his opinion back to the *Enterprise* in an article entitled "The Menken—Written Especially for Gentlemen." "She is a finely formed woman down to her knees; if she could be herself that far, and Mrs. H.A. Perry the rest of the way, she would pass for an unexceptionable Venus," he wrote. "Here every tongue sings the praises of her matchless grace, her supple gestures, her charming attitudes. Well, possibly, these tongues are right . . . She don't talk well, and as she goes on her shape and her acting, the character of a fidgety 'dummy' is peculiarly suited to her line of business."

Adah Menken and her striptease electrified San Francisco. In no time at all she was clasped to the bosom of the *Golden Era* crowd, and her poetry began appearing in that paper—which might not have been the case if she hadn't first achieved her equine-dramatic triumph.

Her success in San Francisco led to a command performance in Virginia City, whence Twain had returned, and on February 27, 1864, she arrived triumphantly in Washoe at the head of an entourage comprised of a troupe of actors, her best friend and fellow Bohemian Ada Clare, Ada's large pack of pet dogs, and Menken's husband, Orpheus C. Kerr, whose real name was Robert H. Newell. She was welcomed with all the pomp Virginia City could muster, and took rooms at the International Hotel, Virginia's most prestigious hostelry.

But what should have been an unalloyed triumph had its dead spots. On her first night at Maguire's Opera House, Menken performed not her old standby *Mazeppa*, but *The French Spy*, a distinctly inferior vehicle in which she appeared fully clothed and had many more lines of dialogue. The audience, made up not of aesthetes and intellectuals, but largely of sweaty and boisterous miners, gave it a resounding thumbs down and hollered for the horse and the flesh-colored suit. The next night they were obliged, and they responded by presenting Menken with a two-thousand-dollar bar of silver duly engraved with the pertinent names and pleasantries.

For the next thirty days Menken remained in Virginia City with her little party, visiting saloons, gambling dens, and brothels, and generally cutting a wide swath through town. The *Enterprise* made much of her visit, reporting her daily activities with a suffused solemnity, for she was a figure, literally and figuratively, of national interest, and the publicity attendant upon her stay in Virginia was of considerable value. Her poetry appeared in the paper on numerous occasions without editorial extrapolations.

Menken had serious literary ambitions. Her husband, Orpheus C. Kerr (his pseudonym amused the Nevadans, who were often besieged by out-of-state "office seekers" casting hopeful eyes upon the territorial government), had been a newspaperman and editor, but Menken made it clear she was after bigger game. She set her sights on Dan De Quille and Mark Twain, star reporters of the *Enterprise* and literary figures of great repute in Nevada and San Francisco. Dan, who was shy, approaching middle age, and married in the bargain, was less alluring than Twain, with his bushy red hair and seductive drawl. Menken was an old hand at this game. She didn't miss an opportunity, whether dropping off a sonnet at the *Enterprise* office or attending a public function, to hang at Twain's elbow, listening raptly to his proclamations. Twain for his part treated her with exaggerated, faintly ironic deference. He referred to her as his "fellow literary cuss" and even submitted some of his sketches for her comment, but he remained a bit aloof nonetheless. Adah, after all, was an adventuress and a Bohemian, and he found both these elements alluring, shady; but she was also Jewish, and that, more than the other attribute, put her in a very questionable category.

Twain had known a few Jews in his native Missouri, and had gone along with the general anti-Semitism that was prevalent in that time and place. He had never stopped to think about it one way or another, as it was a philosophy espoused with equal thoughtlessness by everyone in his walk of life. Much later in his life, when his world view had broadened, he would apologize in print for having been an inadvertent anti-Semite, but in 1863 he had not yet reached that stage in his development. So when Adah Menken let it be known that she was available, all his "moral" scruples surged to the forefront. In addition to his aversion to her religion and her lifestyle, he had never made many bones about the fact that her acting did not impress him. And he found her buxom physique and frizzy golden-red hair a bit too robust for his taste; he preferred slender, pale, spiritual-looking ladies with dark hair. Around Dan, Joe Goodman, and the other *Enterprise* boys, he made nervous jokes about "the Menken's" boisterously existential lifestyle and her thorough lack of morality. Some months later he would thunder self-righteously, in a review of *Mazeppa* in which the lead was taken by another actress, "Let a pure youth witness *Mazeppa* once, and he is pure no longer." One wonders just how he had arrived at that conclusion.

Toward the end of her stay in Virginia City, "the Menken" summoned Mark Twain to a formal dinner in her suite at the International Hotel. Dan De Quille came along, too, either as a chaperon for Twain or to lend the evening a cloak of respectability. Whatever the reason for his presence, it is fortunate that he was there, for he left an engaging account of the proceedings, which were conspicuously absent from Twain's memoirs. He wrote:

"The object of the dinner appeared to be, on Menken's part, a sort of literary consultation. She was full of her proposed novel. Aside from this talk, and some talk of getting up a new play for [Ada] Clare, the dinner was rather dull."

Twain seemed quite ill at ease, De Quille noted, especially since "Mr. Menken," Orpheus C. Kerr, had distinctly not been invited to partake of the Bohemian literary highjinks and could be heard pacing up and down in the hall outside, occasionally poking his head through the door to glower at the revelers. Poor Kerr seems to have been viewed with scorn by the rough-and-tumble male citizenry of California and Nevada, who sneered at "uppity" women but sneered even more at shuffling, apologetic husbands. At any rate, Kerr's days, even as a hanger-on, were numbered: Adah would move on to other triumphs, casting aside the long-suffering Newell for other, more celebrated admirers, including the poet Swinburne and Alexander Dumas *père*.

Unfortunately, this particular evening was not a success, at least according to De Quille's report. Menken and Ada Clare had between them some nineteen dogs of miscellaneous breeds, and these privileged canines lingered near the dinner table, where their mistresses constantly plied them with sugar cubes soaked in brandy and champagne. Twain rapidly grew disgusted with the ill-behaved and increasingly inebriated wolf pack, and so, when one of the creatures took hold of his leg under the table and gave it a playful nip, he aimed a kick in what he perceived was the dog's general direction. Instead he connected with a well-nursed corn on the Menken's foot, "causing her to bound from her seat, throw herself on a lounge and roll and roar in agony."

"This mischance put a sort of damper on the festivities," added De Quille. "Mark immediately became sullen as if it had been his own corn that was wounded, and even when Menken came limping back to her chair and begged him not to mind, he refused to be conciliated." Dan went on to explain that "Mark disliked the Menken and would have avoided the arrangement that seated him by her side had it been possible." However, it is more likely that by this time, the pair's mutual interest was rapidly winding down and what De Quille took as Twain's simple dislike was actually growing disgust—with himself as much as with Menken.

Menken left Virginia City and the West for London shortly afterward. She went on to blaze erratically through the Bohemian firmament in Europe, dying in Paris of pneumonia in 1868 at the age of thirty-three. A slim volume of her histrionic verse, *Infelicia*, was published posthumously. Her friend Ada Clare died of hydrophobia in 1874 after being bitten by one of her pet dogs.

Much could be said about Twain's relationship, however elliptical, with Adah Isaacs Menken. Whether or not his relations with her were sexual is beside the point. What emerges from the accounts of Twain and his contemporaries is that Menken aroused in Twain all sorts of contradictory impulses. The ultimate value of his brief acquaintance with her may very well have been that he was forced to come to terms with his deeply ingrained anti-Semitism. This is not to say that the relationship enabled Twain to overcome his prejudice; he wouldn't reach that point until the last few years of his life, when he wrote an article called "Concerning the Jews" and dictated sections in his autobiography in which he apologized for his past attitudes. But perhaps in being confronted with an attractive woman who also happened to be Jewish, Twain (always a rigorous examiner of his own reactions, even if he wasn't always completely honest in recording them) may have been thrown into some emotional turmoil, spent the following years analyzing the phenomenon, and from that analysis a clearer understanding may eventually have emerged.

There was more to the situation than just Adah's Jewishness, of course. She was a blatantly loose woman, an adventuress who made a career out of shocking people. Twain no doubt found these aspects of her personality exciting, but also offensive to his conventional morality. Ultimately the relationship would never have "gone" anywhere, since Menken was hardly the sort of girl Samuel Clemens could have brought home to mother; but before his Presbyterian conscience got after him, it is likely that Twain had at least a few exciting moments in the company of the era's most celebrated stripper.

True to form, Twain got considerable mileage out of his more socially acceptable romantic relationships—whether in his letters home to his mother and sister, or in his newspaper and magazine pieces. To Jane Clemens and Pamela Moffett he recounted a comedy of errors involving himself and a young woman who was "a relative of Governor Stanford" (and thus, presumably, worthy of his attentions). This changeable specimen of femininity apparently kept him fascinated for a period of several weeks during which he never knew whether she would welcome him with a warm smile or freeze him with an Arctic stare. Finally, he conceded in his letter, he had been forced to give up this roller coaster courtship—it was just "too many for him."

He was also perfectly capable of poking wry fun at himself—or at least a thinly disguised version of himself, in the person of a young San Francisco local reporter named John Brummel. Using his disastrous days on the *Call* as fodder, Twain began work on a play, doomed to remain unfinished, which went by the name *Brummel and Arabella*. He hoped, through theater connections obtained while reviewing plays for the *Dramatic Chronicle*, to see his creation produced, but other things caught his attention, and he never finished it.

The surviving fragment of the play reveals Brummel to be a bumbling, ineffectual fellow whose concentration is apt to wander—a perpetual chaser of news stories that never quite seem to pan out. He is obsessed with longing for the object of his affections, Arabella Webster, and given to pining after her instead of attending to the business at hand. Brummel soliloquizes that it doesn't matter what he's writing—an article about pigs, poultry, conflagrations, or steamboat disasters—he manages to get Arabella mixed into it somehow or other.

> How humiliating it was last night when the chief editor looked over my proof and wanted to know what Arabella Webster it was who was going to fight the prize fight with Rough Scotty the Kentucky Infant. And the day before I had her in three financial notices and drat it, for a week past they haven't sent a pack of old blisters to the county jail for getting on a bender and breaking things but what I've written up the item in a state of semi-consciousness and entire absent-mindedness and added my Arabella's name to the list. This won't do, you know. Some day I'll make a mistake and publish her as arrested for arson, or manslaughter, or shoplifting, or infanticide, or some other little eccentricity of the kind, and she'll notify me to inflict my company and my extraordinary attentions on somebody else.

What can be gathered from Twain's heavy-handed attempt at romantic humor is the fact that his life as a journalist in San Francisco was just too chaotic to permit him to enjoy the ordered pleasures of romance—at least of conventional romance. There were those, such as his journalistic rival Fitz Smythe, who hinted darkly that Twain sought solace in houses of ill repute, a practice which was hardly uncommon for that place and time. Naturally, Twain had nothing to say on the subject. One might wonder whether this was because he considered the practice too common to occasion comment or, more likely, because he was concerned with the stigma attached to such a pastime in the convention-ridden world of the East Coast, and so made it a dark secret of his wayward past. The rumor did come back to haunt him a number of years later when he was courting his future wife, Olivia Langdon, in Elmira, New York, but he managed to get around it somehow.

When Sam Clemens arrived in Nevada in 1861, he still harbored many of the misapprehensions of immaturity, despite his past successful career as a Mississippi pilot. His experiences during the next decade would eliminate nearly all of those misapprehensions. For one thing, he would mature a great deal sexually. In San Francisco and Virginia City he would be forced into contact with women of types he had never seen in Missouri or Illinois—Bohemians, artists, women who stood outside the social confines in which he had been raised. A smalltown boy at heart, he was frankly confused by women such as Ina Coolbrith and Adah Menken. They seemed exotic, even frightening, to a young man like Twain, who had always *thought* the feminine ideal was a rosy-cheeked lass in a sunbonnet, like Laura Wright; or a grave and spiritual young lady given to correcting his faults, like his future wife Olivia Langdon; or perhaps a mixture of the two, like Emeline Beach, whom he would meet a few years later. Writing about women would never be Mark Twain's strong suit. He could handle the subject well enough when he stepped back and viewed women as part of the human race, but the minute he tried to describe them individually he got into trouble and fell back into the old comfortable cliches of sweet, innocent young girls and dignified, motherly women.

Ultimately, Twain would leave these dangerous new types of women behind in the West and seek a more conventional mate in the genteel East. But his experiences with Coolbrith, Menken, and others who went unmentioned were not without fruit. As he learned about the wealth of human experience that he had never observed, much less participated in, back home in Missouri, his subsequent writing would acquire breadth and depth.

As 1865 drew to a close, Twain had other things on his mind besides money and sex. He was often occupied in correcting San Francisco's public servants from the pages of the *Dramatic Chronicle* and the

Enterprise (which enjoyed wide circulation in California). In one of the milder of these epistles, he commented on the novelty of receiving "a neat, voluntary compliment" from the collector of Internal Revenue in San Francisco: a bill for $31.25 in tax on his 1864 income, which had been about $1,650.00. "I am taxed on my income!" he crowed in the *Enterprise*. "This is perfectly gorgeous! I never felt so important in my life before. To be treated in this splendid way, just like another William B. Astor! Gentlemen, we *must* drink." (The federal government had introduced the income tax in 1862 as a temporary measure to drum up funds for the Civil War. Twain, although he went on to pay even greater sums into the federal coffers, never had any other caustic comments to offer on the subject of this peculiarly blatant swindle.)

Always vocal about municipal malfeasance, he continued a series of blistering attacks on San Francisco officials and institutions that had begun when he was reporting for the *Call*. At that time his target was the San Francisco coroner's office, which was being high-handed about giving out information to reporters about death records. The subject of coroners and undertakers had always roused his ire, and he had wielded such a savage pen in his "Petrified Man" satire that he had all but obliterated his subject. Now Twain took San Francisco coroner Massey and his underlings to task in a vitriolic exhortation, one of the only truly passionate and opinionated articles of his which appeared in the *Call*.

> You see the dead-cart leaving the place and ask one of [the coroner's employees] where it is bound, and without looking up from his newspaper, he grunts, lazily, and says, "*Stiff*," meaning that it is going in quest of the corpse of some poor creature whose earthly troubles are over. You ask one of them a dozen questions calculated to throw more light upon a meagre entry in the slate, and he invariably answers, "*Don't know*"—as if the grand end aim of his poor existence was not to know anything, and to come as near accomplishing his mission as his opportunities would admit . . . One of these fellows said to us yesterday, "We have taken away the slate; we are not going to give you any more information; the reporters have got too sharp— by George, they known more'n *we* do!" God help the reporter that

don't! It is as fervent a prayer as ever welled up from the bottom of our heart.

The diatribe succeeded in humbling the arrogant Massey, who thereafter allowed San Francisco journalists all the information they wanted. But Twain wasn't satisfied—not by a long shot. When Benjamin Sheldon, the coroner of the city's branch office, died four days after the publication of the *Call* attack, Twain lobbied long and hard to get Dr. Stephen R. Harris elected in his place. "I went into the Board of Supervisors & button-holed every member & worked like a slave for my man," he wrote his mother and sister. "When I began he hadn't a friend in the Board. He was elected just like a knife, & Mr. Massey is out in the cold."

Another favorite target was Martin G. Burke, San Francisco's police chief. The San Francisco police department was notoriously corrupt, and other reporters besides Twain attacked it in vituperative articles. But Twain, as usual, was right out in front—at least, he seemed to be having more fun than the other reporters when he vilified San Francisco's finest and their bloated chief. The fact that he was correct in his assessment of the force's corruption was no protection, and eventually, after several of the accusatory missives had appeared in the *Enterprise*, Burke filed a libel suit against the paper. This goaded Twain into responding with another, more blistering attack, in which he accused the police of aiding and abetting lecherous practices in the city by turning a (paid-for) blind eye to them. He was fully aware of the danger inherent in his attacks; on the envelope in which he mailed the article to Virginia City, he scrawled a note to the *Enterprise* print shop: "Be sure and let Joe see this before it goes in." When Goodman read the cutting diatribe, his only reply was, "Let it all go in, every word. If Mark can stand it, I can."

This was the state of affairs when Twain became involved in an unfortunate situation with Steve Gillis. Roommates and bosom buddies, Twain and Gillis often terrorized nocturnal San Francisco, sometimes in the company of "Little" Ward. Twain, it should be remarked, had never been one for physical combat, either hand-to-hand or with firearms, preferring to conduct his battles with verbal ammunition. Unlike his more cerebral roommate, Gillis was always on the lookout for a scrap.

One night shortly after the lawsuit had been initiated against the *Enterprise*, Gillis was on his way home from work at the *Call* when he spotted a saloon brawl in progress on Howard Street. On closer inspection, it turned out to have elements that made getting involved in it worthwhile. Apparently the saloon's proprietor, a ruffian called Big Jim Casey, had just settled back to enjoy the spectacle of a muscular thug making mincemeat out of a small and defenseless party who just happened to be an enemy of Casey.

Gillis was familiar with the principals in the little drama, and when he had ascertained the scenario, he promptly leaped into the fray in defense of the underdog. Big Jim, as might be expected, did not take very kindly to this unscheduled change in the evening's festivities, and he stepped in and broke up the fight, allowing the underdog to crawl away. Then Casey locked the front door to the saloon, put the only key in his pocket, and turned to face Gillis. "Now, Mister, since you've butted in without being asked, I'll finish the job on you," he snarled, lunging at Gillis. But Steve managed to snatch a large, heavy glass beer pitcher off the bar, and the minute the enraged Casey got within striking distance, Gillis hit him over the head with the massive object. The cut glass produced in those days was certainly more substantial than it is today, for as a result of the blow the big bruiser crumpled onto the sawdust-covered floor, unconscious.

Steve Gillis now attempted to leave the scene of the crime, but that proved impossible. The key to the door was in Casey's pocket, and the massive Casey was lying upon it. Gillis was still standing in front of the long mahogany bar, feverishly pondering possible avenues of escape, when two constables broke down the door in response to a call. Seeing Big Jim lying on the floor with blood streaming copiously from his scalp, the officers decided to arrest Gillis first and ask questions later. He was conveyed roughly and unceremoniously to the police station (an edifice described by Twain as "the infernalest smelling den on earth, perhaps"), where he was charged with assault and battery and locked up until somebody should arrive to bail him out.

That task fell to Mark Twain. When he heard that Gillis was behind bars, Twain managed to scrape together the five hundred dollars needed for his bail. Then Twain dragged Gillis home, blasting him mercilessly for getting into such a scrape. Didn't Steve realize how precarious a position Twain was going to be in, what with his already cordial relations vis-à-vis Burke and the constabulary?

The next day, Twain and Gillis received a piece of news that made their blood run cold—Big Jim Casey's condition had worsened, and he was raving deliriously over in the county hospital. The general consensus was that the next saloon Casey would be operating would be located somewhere on the outskirts of the Elysian fields— if he wasn't dispensing drink in a warmer climate. Casey, it should be pointed out, was a special friend of Chief of Police Burke. Thus, when he shuffled his mortal coil, as it seemed he would, both Twain and Gillis were more than likely to be in hot water—or perhaps rope—up to their necks.

Reflecting briefly, Gillis decided to become a bail jumper. He would abscond to Virginia City and resume his position as a typesetter for the *Enterprise*. As for Twain, the pleasures of San Francisco were becoming a little contemptible from over-familiarity. So he planned to take a vacation, and consequently avoid implication in the charge of Gillis's bail jumping as well as the more undesirable consequences that might result from the lawsuit. Steve's older brother Jim Gillis happened to be visiting in San Francisco at the time of the Casey episode, and he graciously offered Twain sanctuary in his cabin in the Mother Lode mining country on the Stanislaus River, some two hundred miles southeast of San Francisco. So on December 4, 1865, Twain took up his residence in Jim Gillis's cabin on Jackass Hill, and hunkered down for the winter.

6

The Society Upon
the Stanislaus

In his own way, Jim Gillis was quite literary. He lived in a cabin on Jackass Hill, not far from the Mother Lode mining towns of Tuttle-town and Sonora, surrounded by sighing pines and in full view of the regal Sierra Nevada range. The great Stanislaus River, which was to be immortalized in "The Society Upon the Stanislaus" and other writings of Bret Harte, came rushing down from the heights of the Sierra, ending its dash as a silver stream where miners set up sluice boxes. Harte had spent a brief period living in Jim Gillis's cabin during the 1850s, at a time when his fortunes were at their lowest ebb. Ill, penniless, and discouraged about his future, he had accepted a twenty-dollar gold piece from Gillis as well as his advice to try his luck on a San Francisco newspaper. A few months later, during a visit to San Francisco, Gillis found out Harte's where-abouts and dropped in on him just to see how he was getting on. Harte took offense at Gillis's visit, assuming that his benefactor was merely trying to get back the twenty dollars he had lent him. He sent Gillis away rather perfunctorily, refusing to listen when Gillis tried to explain that he had written off the debt and was there merely to congratulate Harte on the fact that he seemed to be making a successful career for himself in the city.

JIM GILLIS'S CABIN ON JACKASS HILL IN CALIFORNIA'S MOTHER
LODE COUNTRY. THE CABIN SEEN HERE LATER BURNED DOWN,
AND A NEW ONE WAS BUILT AROUND THE ORIGINAL STONE CHIM-
NEY, WHICH SURVIVED THE FIRE.

Twain arrived at Jackass Hill on December 4. He found Gillis's retreat Spartan but aesthetic, with "no planking on the floor; old bunks, pans and traps of all kinds—Byron, Shakespeare, Bacon, Dickens & every kind of only first class literature," as he wrote in the notebook he was keeping at the time. The abundance of books was indicative of Gillis's propensity for self-education; despite his isolation, Jim kept up with the outside world by subscribing to daily and weekly newspapers as well as perusing works of literature. He had a reputation for Solomon-like wisdom among the denizens of Jackass Gulch, Angels Camp, and the surrounding vicinity, and they often brought him disputes to settle.

The area surrounding Angels Camp had been a populous mining settlement during the flush period of the 1850s, but by the time Twain took up his temporary abode on Jackass Hill, only a handful of dilapidated cabins occupied the spot where, twelve or fifteen years earlier, a vital, thriving boom town had been conducting its bustling business. Twain later recalled the area as "that serene and reposeful and dreamy and delicious sylvan paradise," but he was also struck by the lost and bygone air of the dead mining camp. It struck a chord in Twain, for it symbolized just how mercurial life and fortune in the West could be. The ghostly ruins of Angels Camp caught his fancy as he loafed and dreamed among them; it seemed to him that the green hillside, with its collapsing cabins and bare foundations, suited his present mood exactly. "The mere handful of miners still remaining had seen the town spring up, spread, grow, and flourish in its pride; and they had seen it sicken and die, and pass away like a dream," he wrote in *Roughing It.* "With it their hopes had died, and their zest of life . . . It was the most singular, and almost the most touching and melancholy exile that fancy can imagine. One of my associates in this locality [perhaps Jim Gillis], for two or three months, was a man who had had a university education; but now for eighteen years he had decayed there by inches, a bearded, rough-clad, clay-stained miner, and at times, among his sighings and soliloquizings, he unconsciously interjected vaguely remembered Latin and Greek sentences—dead and musty tongues, meet vehicles for the thoughts of one whose dreams were all of the past, whose life was a failure; a tired man, burdened with the present and indifferent to the future; a man without ties, hopes, interests, waiting for rest and the end." More than Jim Gillis, Twain may have been thinking of himself, mingling pathos and autobiography with a free hand.

He and Jim Gillis shared the cabin with Jim's younger brother Billy, and with a miner named Dick Stoker, "grave and simple . . . forty-six, gray as a rat, earnest, thoughtful, slenderly educated, slouchily dressed and clay-soiled, but his heart was finer metal than any gold his shovel ever brought to light—than any, indeed, that ever was mined or minted," as Twain was to describe him in *Roughing It.* Stoker, Jim Gillis, and the few remaining miners in the area engaged in what was known as "pocket" mining—a process that was unique to that one small corner of California, at least as far as Twain knew. After spending a few months in the apparent capital of pocket mining, Twain was to claim that it was the most fascinating style of prospecting he had ever witnessed—perhaps, as he observed, because, due to its extreme uncertainty, pocket mining sent a large number of victims to the lunatic asylum.

The theory behind pocket mining was that in this particular part of California, gold was scattered at random throughout the soil, and the only thing needed to pinpoint precisely where it lay was a systematic method. The pinpointing was accomplished through a tedious process of panning the soil in random increments. Perhaps a few panfuls of earth, when rinsed with water, would reveal tiny flecks of gold; if so, then the prospector would try samples from either side of the lucky strike to narrow down his field of search. By this process of elimination, the miner would eventually hope to locate the section where the most gold was concentrated. It was by nature both labor-intensive and time-consuming, and not even an old hand at pocket mining like Jim Gillis or Dick Stoker could readily foresee the result. Sometimes a pocket miner would strike one initial shovelful of gold and then never come up with any more, no matter how diligently he searched. There were, however, good reasons for the pocket miners to keep up their work. One strike, for instance, had been made in the area not long before Twain arrived, and had totalled sixty-thousand dollars worth of gold. It had taken two men two weeks to dig out the bonanza; they then sold the excavation site for ten thousand dollars to another fellow who, according to Twain, never got fifty dollars out of it afterward.

Twain was as fascinated as ever with the concept of sudden wealth, but his energy was at a low ebb and he was content to leave the physical work to those with broader shoulders and fewer qualms about labor than he. His roommates loved to rib him about his lassitude, which rapidly became legendary among them. He could be teased, cajoled, bullied into accompanying Jim or Dick to a promising mining site, but he much preferred to linger by the fireplace in the cabin, reading, scribbling in his notebook, or composing mysterious opuses on foolscap paper, which he would then insist on reading aloud to his cabin mates. (They did not stand on ceremony when it came to deflating his literary pretensions, Steve Gillis recalled some years later.)

But one raw, drizzly afternoon, Jim managed to drag Twain up a hill to a likely prospecting spot. The weather was nasty, and probably inspired a remark Twain recorded in his notebook: "Couldn't been colder if I had swallowed an ice-berg." Once they set to work, Gillis, who was well versed in the vagaries of pocket mining, became convinced that they were about to make a big strike any minute. Twain was less sure, but arguing took too much effort, so he kept his doubts to himself. His job was to fetch water from a stream that was flowing at the foot of the hill; the water was then used to wash the pans of dirt to uncover any specks of gold. As the afternoon progressed, each pan looked more promising than the one before it, but by the time gray twilight began to descend, there had still been no payoff, and meanwhile Twain was shivering miserably and his teeth were chattering as the drizzle soaked through his clothes. Finally he drawled, "Jim, I won't carry any more water. This work is too disagreeable."

Poor Jim was just about to wash out another pan of soil when he received this ultimatum. "Bring one more pail, Sam," he pleaded.

But Twain was obstinate. He was cold right through to the bones; he was going to hike back home forthwith. In vain did Gillis repeat his request in a beseeching tone of voice. "Just one more pail, Sam?"

THE MINER'S DREAM.

"No sir, not a drop, not even if I knew there were a million dollars in that pan."

Sadly, Gillis ceased his laboring, for he couldn't simultaneously fetch water and wash dirt by himself. After posting the required thirty-day claim at the site, they walked back downhill to the cabin.

The weather prevented them from engaging in any further prospecting on the site, and they soon forgot about the hillside claim altogether and moved on to other locations. Meanwhile, the rain had washed away the topsoil in the pan of earth they had left behind at the claim—the pan that Twain had refused to fetch the water to wash. Under the topsoil in that pan, as it turned out, was a handful of solid gold nuggets.

This was naturally likely to catch the eye of miners more enterprising than Mark Twain. Two Austrians happened along, spied the glittering lure in the pan, and sat down to wait until Gillis's thirty-day claim had expired. As soon as it had, they began panning the surrounding earth with feverish intensity. Two or three pans of dirt later they struck a pocket of nuggets. By the time they had cleaned it out, they were twenty thousand dollars richer.

In San Francisco, Twain had been accustomed to dining on scalloped oysters and champagne beneath the gilt chandeliers of elegant, quasi-European restaurants. In Angels Camp, where he frequented the local drinking and dining establishments, the victuals were bound to be considerably less refined. He made the following note in his journal: "Jan. 23, 1865—Angels—Rainy, stormy—Beans & dishwater for breakfast at the Frenchman's; dishwater & beans for dinner, and both articles warmed over for supper."

After a few more days of rain, beans, and dishwater, his grumbling took on a somewhat brighter note: "26th—Tapidaro [the leather covering on a saddle] beefsteak for a change—no use, could not bite it."

"28th—Chili beans & dishwater three times to-day, as usual, & some kind of 'slum' which the Frenchman called 'hash.' Hash be d——d."

There was a happy ending, of sorts.

"30th Jan. Moved to new hotel, just opened—good fare, & coffee that a Christian may drink without jeopardizing his eternal soul."

Twain was busy improving himself in his exile, studying French (which he practiced on the aforementioned French hotelier—ostensibly this did not occasion the dubious cuisine which irked him so) and music, as his journal indicates: "Lesson VI," a simple little waltz reproduced laboriously on crooked hand-drawn staff lines, indicates that his pianistic development was embryonic.

After the sophisticated society of San Francisco, Twain found Angels Camp's small population just as tedious as the grub. He was, not surprisingly, often bored to tears by the local goings-on, which probably reminded him of the backwoods settlements in Missouri and Illinois. He noted sourly in his journal the following event in the lives of his Jackass Hill neighbors, the Carringtons: "The exciting topic of conversation in this sparse community just at present (and it always *is* in dire commotion about something or other of small consequence), is Mrs. Carrington's baby, which was born a week ago, on the 14th. There was nothing remarkable about the baby, but if Mrs. C had given birth to an ornamental cast-iron dog big enough for an embellishment for the State-House steps I don't believe the event would have created more intense interest in the community." Most of the nearby residents were of the caliber of Mrs. Slasher, whom Twain described as "Englishwoman 45 years old—married merchant of 38—wears breeches—foulmouthed b——h. Tom found her blackguarding little Mrs. S last night, had her cornered & holding her two small children behind her. Said she—'An don't I know you—you're only a common strumpet & both them brats is bastards. And here is Mr. Tom will say the same.' Tom said she was a distempered d——d old slut & recommended a dose of scalding water for her. The little woman's husband came in at this juncture, & mildly begged Mrs Slasher to go home until she was sober. She turned on him & said he was a rounder & had gotten a bastard by a Wallah. Tom suggested that the d——d old pelter be bundled neck & crop into the creek."

The only locals Twain could tolerate were a nearby family with two young and comely daughters, Molly and Nelly Daniels, "who boasted of having the slimmest waists, the largest bustles, and the stiffest starched petticoats in the whole locality." Twain and Billy Gillis often paid formal calls on these "Chaparral Quails," as they were known. Billy paired off with Molly, while Twain favored Nelly—in fact, Jim Gillis imagined Twain married to her, "grubbing around on the hillside for bark." (Nelly may have prompted Twain to complain in his journal about the "d——d girl always reading novels like [Ned Buntline's] 'The Convict, Or The Conspirator's Daughter', & going into ecstasies about them to her friends.")

The foursome was fond of walks along the deserted trails that disappeared into the hills. On one of these occasions, the party got lost in those hills and came straggling home to the Daniels's cabin at an hour that was too late to be considered proper. Mrs. Daniels assailed them at the door with harsh words about heedless rakes such as Twain, who would stoop so low as to seduce young and innocent girls in cow pastures. Twain wisely refused to involve himself in this one-sided conversation, and, walking over to a corner of the cabin, he picked up a guitar that was leaning against the wall and proceeded to sing and play a few songs called forth from memory. (He always loved simple tunes, especially black spirituals, which he had heard from birth.) Mrs. Daniels was so thoroughly enchanted by this musical interlude, which reminded her of her old life "back in the States," that she wound up cooking a late supper for the prodigal minstrel, Billy Gillis, and her daughters.

One of the things Twain enjoyed the most about living on Jackass Hill was listening to Jim Gillis tell tall tales in front of the fireplace on chilly afternoons and evenings. Gillis would adopt a reflective stance, hands crossed behind him and back to the fire, and proceed to relate elaborate and ultimately implausible tales, usually featuring Dick Stoker as their hero. Meanwhile Stoker would sit quietly in a corner, smoking his pipe and nodding serenely as Gillis painted him in increasingly fantastic lights. One of Gillis's yarns, retold by Twain in *Roughing It*, was about the remarkable sagacity of Stoker's cat, Tom Quartz. It didn't matter that Stoker did not own a cat and had never owned one; Gillis went on describing the feline's perspicacity in mining as if the animal were fresh in his mind from the day before. Another Gillis tale, "The Tragedy of the Burning Shame," found its way into *Huckleberry Finn* as the "Royal Nonesuch" episode. Twain regretted that he had to clean up the yarn considerably to make it fit for publication. "This was a great damage," he mourned in his *Autobiography*. "As Jim told it, inventing it as he went along, I think it was one of the most outrageously funny things I have ever listened to. How mild it is in the book and how pale; how extravagant and gorgeous in its unprintable form!" Twain also mined his Mother Lode experiences in the short story "The Californian's Tale," which appeared in *Harper's* magazine in 1902, and described a widowed miner in a back-country cabin who had lost his grip on reality with the loss of his wife.

When plagued with cabin fever, Twain, sometimes with Jim or Dick Stoker, would drift down the hill into Angels Camp, where they frequented the Tryon Tavern, later part of the Angels Camp Hotel. Twain long remembered the slanting, battered relic of a pool table in the tavern. In his old age his fancy sometimes returned to its torn felt and undulating surface, its chipped balls and headless cues "with curves in them like parentheses." Once Twain, Gillis, and Stoker saw their fellow tavern habitué, Texas Tom, rack up a whopping total of seven points during a single turn, and they all went mad with admiration and amazement.

The bartender, Ben (or Ross, as some accounts have it) Coons, was a young, dapper bartender with yellowish brown sideburns; he was a former Illinois River pilot, and fond of telling long, pointless tales. Twain later described him as "a dull person, and ignorant; he had no gift as a story-teller, and no invention." Coons delivered these monologues straight-faced and unsmiling, as if he were imparting solid wisdom and intended his listeners to take notes. Later, Twain would write on several occasions about people to whom all details were of equal importance. It is likely that the granddaddy of all these infuriating droners was the self-important Coons.

One raw and dreary afternoon, Coons began soliloquizing about a frog belonging to some man named Coleman. Coleman, it seemed, had trained this frog to jump on command, but when he tried to pit it against another frog, the rival's owner secretly loaded

Coleman's amphibian with buckshot, weighing it down and causing it to lose the contest. This was a witless enough story, and Coons had in all probability stumbled across it in one of the area newspapers (at least three Mother Lode papers would later claim to have first published the jumping frog anecdote, usually at some time during the 1850s). Coons may even have heard the story on the river, for it was far from original. But it was Coons's uniquely irritating delivery rather than the yarn itself that struck Twain as noteworthy. He jotted down the bare bones of the story in his notebook, intending to go back to it and some point and write it up more fully. "Coleman with his jumping frog—bet stranger $50—stranger had no frog, & C got him one—in the meantime stranger filled C's frog full of shot & he couldn't jump—the stranger's frog won."

The two months Twain spent in the Mother Lode were extremely fruitful for his writing. With no daily journalistic grind, and a number of interesting sources of potential material, he was able to relax, absorb, and digest. Occasionally he tried his hand at a little sketch, such as the "Report of Prof. G——to accompany Map & Views of the Great Vide Poche [i.e., Empty Pocket] Mine, on Mount Olympus, Calaveras Co." This was a full-blown article written, as the title suggests, in the form of a report by some self-appointed mining expert (very likely Jim Gillis) to an undisclosed committee. Twain probably composed it for delivery to the nightly gathering in the cabin. From long immersion in the jargon of mining, with its dips and sinuosities, and his experience in the filibuster-ridden Nevada Territorial Legislature, Clemens had acquired the ability to lampoon pompous sounding claptrap, as well as the hifalutin orators who delivered it. This burlesque managed to cram both high-flown terminology and downright scatology into a very limited space. At one point, for instance, "Professor G——" was forced to admit that "The map is not absolutely correct . . . [A]t the time the Prof was drawing it, seated upon a log, he was persistently besieged by piss-ants." The mine's outcroppings were described as containing nearly every mineral known to man: "some soapstone, some brimstone, & even some jackstones, whetstones, 'dobies & brickbats. None of these various articles are found beneath the surface, wherefore the Prof feels satisfied that the [mining] Company have got the world by the ass, since it is manifest that no other organ of the earth's frame could possibly have produced such a dysentery of disorganized & half-digested slumgullion as is here presented."

Although his public humor was developing nicely, Twain remained absolutely humorless when he himself was the target of satire. Billy Gillis recalled many years later that one of the favorite pastimes in the cabin during the long winter evenings was a game in which the "boys" implemented a "Hospital for the Insane" on Jackass Hill. A "board of directors" and "resident physician" were appointed, and reports on particular "patients" were made weekly to the committee by the "physician." When Twain's turn as "physician" rolled around, he expressed his grave and fatherly concern about the condition of James N. Gillis, "a companionable young fellow [who] tells some fairly humorous stories . . . [I]t is sad to know that this young man, who would otherwise be a useful member of society, is hopelessly insane, but such, I am sorry to say, is the truth. He is laboring under the illusion that he is the greatest pocket miner on earth. . . . He is a fairly good pocket hunter and knows a gold nugget from a brass door knob, but there are a dozen boys on the hill who can give him cards and spades and beat him at the game."

Jim Gillis laughed just as hard as the others at this "report." The next week, however, it was his turn to be the "physician," and he addressed himself to the problematic case of inmate Samuel L. Clemens.

One of the most pitiful cases of insanity that has ever fallen under my observation is that of a young man named Samuel L. Clemens, who was committed to this hospital on the thirteenth day of last month, from Angels Camp, Calaveras County . . . He has, for the past three years, been associated with newspapermen of rare literary ability. He is obsessed with the idea that they are the spokes of a wheel and himself the hub around which they revolve. He has a mania for story telling, and is at the present time engaged in writing one called "The Jumping Frog of Calaveras," which he imagines will cause his name to be handed down to posterity from generation to generation as the greatest humorist of all time. This great story of his is nothing but a lot of silly drivel about a warty old toad that he was told by some joker in Angels Camp. Every evening when the inmates are together in the living room, he takes up the manuscript and reads to them a page or two of the story . . . Then he will chuckle to himself and murmur about "copyrights" and "royalties." If this was the only trouble with Mark Twain, as he dubs himself in his stories, there would be a reasonable hope of the ultimate restoration of his mentality, but the one great hallucination that will forever bar him from the "busy walks of life" is that he was at one time a pilot on one of the great Mississippi River packets . . . Poor Mark! His nearest approach to being a pilot on the river was when he handled the big steering wheel of a flat boat, freighted with apples from Ohio, which were peddled in towns along the river.

All the "boys" exploded with mirth—all of them, that is, but Twain. He was livid with rage. He leaped to his feet and paced back and forth, flinging out fiery sarcasms at Gillis, and calling the others "a lot of laughing jackals." "I appreciate a joke," he sputtered, "and love fun as much as any boy in the world, but when a lot of rotten stuff like Jim Gillis's funny hash is pulled off on me I am ready to cry quits." As a result of Twain's extreme displeasure, the "asylum" was closed down permanently, although the boys continued to take little pokes at Twain just to hear him rage and curse. "Say, Sam, how many barrels of apples could you load onto that flat-bottomed scow?" they would enquire slyly, and then quickly look around for something to hide behind. Billy Gillis observed that when Twain was angry at someone, instead of talking the incident over in a calm and friendly fashion, he generally grabbed a drill, pick handle, or any other weapon that was handy, and proceeded to brain the offender with it. A similar situation had occurred in Virginia City, when members of the *Enterprise* staff, goaded on by Steve Gillis and Rollin Daggett, had presented Twain with a fake meerschaum pipe in an elaborate public ceremony. Twain, who had thanked the "boys" with a stirring and emotional speech, hadn't suspected that the whole thing was a practical joke until he tried to smoke the pipe a few days later, at which time he discovered that, far from being a fine meerschaum, it was a cheap "chalk" monstrosity. Gillis, Daggett, and the others had been well rewarded by Twain's savage response—he was so embarrassed, and consequently angry, that it was weeks before he would even speak to them.

Fortunately for his Jackass Hill cabinmates, Clemens's rages died down as quickly as they flared up, and then he would be likely to suffer great feelings of remorse, although he rarely summoned the fortitude to apologize to the wronged party.

Twain never lost his sensitivity to humor aimed in his direction. An old newspaper clipping which reposes in the files of the Mark Twain Papers at the University of California at Berkeley illustrates this. The article appeared in the Carson City *Appeal* sometime during the 1870s or 1880s. Its author obviously remembered Twain, who was by then on the East Coast, glorying in his reputation as one of America's foremost literary figures. The writer of the squib seemed to want to cut Twain down to size for abandoning the region that had formed him—much as Jim Gillis's "asylum report" had been poking fun at his self-absorption. The *Appeal* piece is a far-fetched, rather labored tale about how Twain and Dan De Quille had taken all the type and other printing equipment "from a recently-defunct newspaper establishment in San Francisco" with which they had presumably been involved, and had headed off to Mendocino to establish a newspaper there. En route, they had purchased a small cannon from a party of emigrants they met, and had then continued on until they finally were forced to stop for the night in a cheerless wilderness area. Late that night (the story continues) they were attacked by hordes of marauding Indians, and Twain, thinking quickly, jumped up and loaded the cannon with "a column of nonpareil and a couple of sticks of young spring poetry," along with some other boilerplate rubbish, which, when shot forth from the cannon, blew the oncoming attackers sky-high and just saved the lives of Mark and Dan by an apostrophe.

The clipping starts off in a serious enough tone, but its absurdity increases steadily, until the article's anonymous composer has the now-famous Twain writing De Quille, years later, from his home in Hartford, Connecticut, and asking Dan to "make a little pilgrimage to that historic spot, gather the ghostly relics together and plant a tablet, not too expensive and at your expense, for the memory of the departed." Its tone is a mixture of De Quille's mechanical hoaxes and Twain's exaggerated style, served up by an admittedly pedestrian scribe who nonetheless hits a few bull's-eyes with his lampoon. Its intent was not lost on Twain, either, for scrawled across the length of the clipping is a message in his handwriting, in purple ink: "Pure imagination—not a fact in it. SLC."

7

A Villainous Backwoods Sketch on Parnassus

During Twain's stay with Jim Gillis, he frequently visited other parts of the Mother Lode. Angels Camp, where Ross Coons had told the tedious frog yarn, was in Calaveras County, while Jackass Hill was located in Tuolumne County. Barely ten miles separated the two places, and Twain covered the area primarily on foot. On New Year's Eve in the Calaveras County hamlet of Vallecito, Twain recorded in his notebook that he had seen a "magnificent lunar rainbow," which he glimpsed through a light, pattering rain. He took it to be an auspicious omen of good fortune, although probably not of the literary variety. Little did he know that his Mother Lode experiences were about to change his life in ways he couldn't have possibly foreseen.

Twain left the Mother Lode country in February 1865, after the winter snows had begun to thaw. He had enjoyed the solitude of the Gillis cabin, and had made numerous jottings in his notebook to record his impressions, but he was pining for civilization, however noisy and chaotic. Word had probably reached him that his hide was no longer hunted in San Francisco, and his funds had run out, so now was as good a time as any to return to the fray.

Bidding Jim and Billy Gillis and Dick Stoker a fond farewell, Twain was riding away on horseback when he discovered that he had left his toothbrush, his pipe, and his pocket knife behind him. He recounted in his notebook how, with much swearing, he was obliged to return and "smouch" Dick Stoker's knife, evidently preferring it to his own.

Resuming his journey, he headed for the boom town of Copperopolis, twelve miles from Jackass Hill, where he could catch the stage to Stockton and thence to San Francisco. Arriving in Copperopolis, he toured the local copper mines, which were nationally famous for their productivity. To his disgust, however, he found that the stage into Stockton would not be leaving that day; he would have to wait until the following morning. He accordingly spent the night in the Copper Hotel, which he dismissed in his notebook as "damned poor," and, catching the stage in the morning, he was in Stockton by 5 P.M. the next day and in San Francisco on the day after, February 26. He promptly checked into the Occidental Hotel—his old "heaven on the entire shell."

As he was signing in, the desk clerk handed him the mail that had come for him during his absence from San Francisco. One of the letters was from Artemus Ward, asking him to send a humorous sketch for a book he was putting together. This was encouraging—except that Ward's letter was dated the previous November. Although Twain had had no real contact with Ward since the "Genial Showman's" wild and woolly tour of Virginia City, the two humorists had kept in touch rather sporadically by letter. In the intervening months, Twain had gradually begun to ponder Ward's advice for him to "leave sage-brush obscurity" for a wider literary fame. He had already submitted articles to the New York *Sunday Mercury*, among other East Coast papers, and had some faint hopes of cracking the national magazine market as well. Ward's request for a witty sketch for inclusion in a book of Nevada Territory travels seemed fortuitous—provided Twain could pull together the requisite item in time.

A couple of days later he wrote to Ward, asking if it were too late to send in a contribution. In early May he received Ward's reply, telling him there was still time to be included in the book, but that Twain should ship the manuscript directly to Carleton and Co., Ward's New York publisher.

Twain did not rush to send anything to Carleton, probably because nothing came immediately to mind. He resumed his contributions to the *Californian*, including articles which touched on his Mother Lode experiences. One of them, "An Unbiased Criticism," published in mid-March, utilized a Coons-like character, called Simon Wheeler, as a narrator. "Wheeler," like Coons, was prone to lengthy, disconnected expostulations, delivered in a painfully slow monotone. During visits to Bret Harte's editorial sanctum, Twain entertained him by imitating this tedious style of speech while relating the jumping frog anecdote he had heard in Angels Camp. Harte was charmed, and suggested that Twain write up the yarn.

For all its simplicity, the jumping frog seems to have eluded Twain's narrative grasp. Between September and October of 1865, he attempted, and discarded without finishing, two prototypical jumping frog sketches. He was frustrated by the fluidity of Coons's spoken monologue, which, no matter how he struggled, refused to be reduced to mere print. Meanwhile, Artemus Ward continued to send follow-up letters, imploring Twain to throw together an article and ship it to Carleton posthaste.

In addition to the purely technical difficulties he faced in the composition of the story, Twain was suffering internal conflicts during this period. His contributions to the *Californian* show that he was doing his best to make the transition from "mere" humorist to "moral statistician," a transition he seemed to feel was necessary if he were to move from regional humorist to national man of letters. Humorous squibs were fine for the *Enterprise* or the *Golden Era*, but the journals and book publishers of the East Coast, the benchmark of literary reputations, required weightier material. Twain's sense of moral rectitude had been with him since childhood, but his ability to create satire rather than humor was still in its developmental stage, as evinced by some of his more ponderous articles in the *Californian*. Artemus Ward's request for a humorous frontier tale no doubt brought on mixed emotions: here was his chance to reach a wide national audience, but with an inferior sort of vehicle. Twain liked and admired Ward, but privately admitted to some reservations about his backwoods style of humor, which relied on misspellings and grammatical outrages to achieve its effect. Twain had higher aspirations for his work. As he struggled with the frog story, he may have hoped he would miss Ward's deadline altogether, and thereby avoid being lumped together with other "phunny phellows" and tarred with the same brush.

Finally, on October 16, he began writing a third version, "Jim Smiley and His Jumping Frog." He finished it in two days and rushed with it to the offices of the Pacific Mail line, entrusting it to the liner *Golden City*. It arrived in New York on November 10, too late to be included in *Artemus Ward: His Travels*, which had already been printed and bound and was officially announced on November 11. George Carleton, the book's publisher, sent the article on to Henry Clapp, editor of the New York *Sunday Press*, who was familiar with Twain's writings from West Coast periodicals.

The *Press* had begun as the newsletter of Pfaff's coffeehouse in Greenwich Village, the nerve center of East Coast Bohemianism. For a period, sodden with absinthe and exaggerated posturings, the publication had threatened to die "of its own Bohemian excesses and dissipations," but a revival "under apparently more moral auspices, and in respectable quarto form"—probably fueled by an infusion of cash—had rescued it from oblivion. Artemus Ward was one of its star contributors. On November 18, Clapp published "Jim Smiley and His Jumping Frog," with the following introduction: "We give up the principal portion of our editorial space, to-day, to an exquisitely humorous sketch . . . by Mark Twain, who will shortly become a regular contributor to our columns. Mark Twain is the assumed name of a writer in California who has long been a favorite contributor to the San Francisco press, from which his articles have been so extensively copied as to make him nearly as well known as Artemus Ward."

During the next month, "Jim Smiley and His Jumping Frog" met with a similar fate. It was widely reprinted throughout the East Coast. Richard Ogden, the New York correspondent for the San

Francisco *Alta California*, reported that it had "set all New York in a roar . . . I have been asked fifty times about it and its author . . . It is voted the best thing of the day." He went on, "Cannot the *Californian* afford to keep Mark all to itself? It should not let him scintillate so widely without first being filtered through the California press."

Twain's own reaction to his sudden fame, or notoriety, was rather mixed. In a letter to his mother and sister, he wrote, "I don't know what to write—my life is so uneventful. I wish I was back there piloting up & down the river again. Verily, all is vanity and little worth—save piloting." Then he dropped his disaffected stance and got down to business: "To think that after writing many an article a man might be excused for thinking tolerably good, those New York people should single out a villainous backwoods sketch to compliment me on! 'Jim Smiley & His Jumping Frog'—a squib which would never have been written but to please Artemus Ward, & then it reached New York too late to appear in his book. But no matter—his book was a wretchedly poor one, generally speaking, & it could be no credit to either of us to appear between its covers." He glued the paragraph from the *Alta* onto the page, and then went on.

Bret Harte & I have both quit the "Californian." He will write for a Boston paper hereafter, [the Boston *Christian Register*] and I for the "New York Weekly Review" and possibly for the "Saturday Press" sometimes . . . Though I am generally placed at the head of my breed of scribblers in this part of the country, the place properly belongs to Bret Harte, I think, . . . though he denies it, along with the rest. He wants me to club a lot of old sketches together with a lot of his, & publish a book together. I wouldn't do it, only he agrees to take all the trouble. But I want to know whether we are going to make anything out of it first, however. He has written to a New York publisher, & if we are offered a bargain that will pay for a month's labor, we will go to work & prepare the volume for the press. My labor will not occupy more than 24 hours, because I will only have to take the scissors & slash my old sketches out of the Enterprise & the Californian—I burned up a small cart-load of them lately—so *they* are forever ruled out of any book—but they were not worth republishing . . . And we have got another secret on hand. We are going to burlesque a book of poems which the publisher, Bancroft, is to issue in the spring. We know all the tribe of California poets, & understand their different styles, & I think we can just make them get up & howl. If Bancroft prints his book in New York in the spring, ours shall be in press there at the same time, & come out promptly with his volume. Then you'll hear these poetical asses here tear around worse than a pack of wild-cats . . . I am willing enough to go into this thing, because there will be *fun* in it.

The letter went on to outline, although in vague terms, another possible book project he was considering, described in an enclosed clipping as being "on an entirely new subject, one that has not been written about heretofore." This subject of this mysterious book was the Mississippi River, but it wouldn't see print until 1875, as *Life on the Mississippi*.

He was growing sick of the West, itching to leave "this accursed homeless desert." Shortly after the publication of "Jumping Frog," he heard that a business acquaintance, Herman Camp, was leaving for the East Coast and was willing to act as the Clemens family's agent in selling thirty thousand acres of land in Tennessee, John Clemens's legacy. Twain asked Camp to advance him a thousand dollars so he could travel to New York and assist him with the sale—thinking, of course, of the publishing connections he could make while he was there. But when Camp agreed to buy the Tennessee land for two-hundred thousand dollars, with a view toward planting the acreage in wine grapes, Orion, who had re-cently become a temperance supporter, was suddenly seized with a fit of morality. He vowed he would never sell the land to debauchers of men who profited from the evil draughts of Bacchus, and the sale was killed. His brother was forced to remain in the "accursed homeless desert," with those evil draughts his only consolation, no doubt.

As it turned out, none of Twain's book projects would fare much better, at least for the time being. The "collected sketches" of Twain and Bret Harte fell by the wayside, although Twain's first book, *The Celebrated Jumping Frog of Calaveras County, and Other Sketches*, would be published in 1867; the poetical parody appears to have been a passing fancy. But there was excitement on the horizon nonetheless. In his postscript Twain referred in passing to the steamer *Ajax*, which had just departed for a month-long trip to the Sandwich Islands carrying fifty-two passengers, "the cream of the town— gentlemen & ladies both, & a splendid brass band." He explained that he had been invited on the voyage, but that he couldn't accept "because there would be no one to write my correspondence while I was gone." (He was still writing a daily letter for the *Enterprise* in addition to his other freelance work.) He went on, "But I am so sorry now. If the *Ajax* were back I would go—quick!—and throw up the correspondence. Where could a man catch such another crowd together?"

That postscript pointed into the future: in two months Twain would be on board the *Ajax*, headed for the Sandwich Islands, minus the brass band and the select crowd, but bound for a new chapter in his career.

8

"Our Fellow Savages of the Sandwich Islands"

In early February 1866, Mark Twain made a brief junket to Sacramento to report on that city for the *Enterprise*. He arrived in California's capital at three A.M. one morning "in company with several other disreputable characters," he wrote, "on board the good steamer *Antelope*, Captain Poole, commander."

The increasingly restless Twain found some respite during the boat trip through the Oakland estuary, past San Pablo, around Suisun Bay and into the Sacramento Delta. Sacramento, then as now, was distinctly provincial compared with the gaudiness of San Francisco, but it was a change of scenery, and Twain appreciated it as such. True to character, his first impression of the state capital was that it was "the City of Saloons." "I know I am departing from usage in calling Sacramento the City of Saloons instead of the City of the Plains," he apologized in his first article, "but I have my justification—I have not found any plains here, yet, but I have been in most of the saloons, and there are a good many of them. You can shut your eyes and march into the first door you come to and call for a drink, and the chances are that you will get it."

Then Twain remembered that he was supposed to be describing

some of the other things in Sacramento for his *Enterprise* readers, so he included a "Brief Climate Paragraph": "This is the mildest, balmiest, pleasantest climate one can imagine. The evenings are especially delightful—neither too warm nor too cold. I wonder if it is always so?"

Following this obligatory attention to detail, he returned to subjects closer to his heart, such as relations with the proprietor of his hotel, "a large, fine-looking man, with a chest which must have made him a most powerful man before it slid down." He and Twain apparently had a number of disagreements, for in an article entitled "I Try to Out 'Sass' the Landlord—And Fail," Twain recorded the following exchange of pleasantries:

"Old Smarty from Mud Springs, I apprehend," Twain hissed within the innkeeper's hearing.

"Young Lunar Caustic from San Francisco, no doubt," the proprietor snarled back.

Some of Twain's *Enterprise* articles were reprinted in the Sacramento *Union*, and were received by the Sacramentans with much appreciation. Forthwith, the gears of inspiration began to grind in Twain's mind. He didn't particularly want to return to San Francisco and continue his correspondence there, having tired of the same predictable existence in one place. He knew that the *Ajax* was planning another voyage to the Sandwich Islands and was determined to be aboard when it went.

Twain reported to *Union* publishers James Anthony and Paul Morrill, bright, early, and presumably sober, and laid before them his plan. The Sandwich Islands, with their sugar industry, were beginning to mean a great deal to California's economy; they were thus a newsworthy subject. Furthermore, the islands' scenery and the customs of their savages would make fascinating reading—in the *Union*. The trifling sum his passage aboard the *Ajax* would cost would be well worth the series of daily articles he would send back to them.

For reasons best known to themselves, Anthony and Morrill acquiesced to Twain's proposal. It certainly wasn't going to do the *Union* any harm to have the man who was rapidly becoming California's most celebrated writer serving as their Sandwich Islands correspondent—not at that price, anyway.

When Twain received the green light, all his ennui and depression vanished immediately, leaving only a little alcoholic vapor behind. He threw himself into an orgy of further travel planning, figuring that once he was back from the islands, he would head straight across the continental United States: up the Columbia River, through Montana, and down the Missouri River to his boyhood home. It didn't much matter to him whether or not he would ever complete, or even begin, the ambitious trip he had outlined for himself—it was the *idea* of travel that had caught his fancy at the moment.

On March 5 he wrote to his mother and sister, "I start to do the Sandwich Islands day after tomorrow . . . I am to remain there a month and ransack the islands, the great cataracts and the volcanoes completely, and write twenty or thirty letters to the Sacramento *Union*—for which they pay me as much money as I would get if I staid at home."

Meanwhile, other observers were also commenting on Twain's travel plans in the public prints. Fitz Smythe, writing for the Nevada Gold Hill *Evening News* under the name "Amigo," had been for some time hinting darkly that Twain's private life was a questionable commodity. For one thing, said "Amigo," the "Bohemian from the sage-brush" had "lost $40 in the house of a lady, under peculiar circumstances." Twain, he went on, "had also lost his watch in the aforementioned establishment," though "he thought the police had stolen it on the night previous, having been oblivious to the fact that his friend had taken it from him early in the evening, in order to save him from loss." Finally, Evans got down to brass tacks, expostulating that Twain "probably had a venereal disease." He continued to report on Clemens's medical history, observing a couple of weeks later, "I understand that [Mark Twain] . . . is disgusted with San Francisco. Well, my boy, that disgust is mutual, and I don't wonder that he wants to leave . . . He has been a little out of health of late and is now endeavoring to get a chance to go to Honolulu, where he expects to get rid of one disease by catching another; the last being more severe for the time being, but more readily yielding to medical treatment . . . If he goes he will be sadly missed by the police, but then they can stand it."

Evans may have had some proof that Twain had contracted syphilis or gonorrhea; Clemens's letters and journals for the next several months refer to a feeling of general debility, some of which can be explained by various ailments he picked up during his travels; but its ultimate cause must remain a mystery. It is not surprising that Twain, as a reporter in Virginia City and San Francisco, had spent time in houses of ill repute as well as saloons, station houses, jails, and gambling dens. Syphilis was common on the frontier, where the bulk of the male population was single, rootless, and deprived of conventional female companionship; effective treatments were severely limited, and often the stigma attached to having a "social disease" kept sufferers from seeking medical advice. Perhaps because he had been a sickly child, tortured by well-meaning but ignorant and ineffectual physicians, Twain never had much respect for doctors, preferring self-treatment with homeopathic remedies. If indeed he did have syphilis symptoms, he kept them to himself and did not consult a physician. He may have been unaware that he had contracted the disease, as its early symptoms are often so slight as to be unnoticeable; or he may have known he had it but was too embarrassed to admit it and chose to suffer in silence. Given Fitz Smythe's heavy-handedness as a satirist and his self-imposed role as defender of the police force, it is more likely that he was merely trying to hit below the belt, as it were, in ridiculing Twain, rather than describing actualities. There are no other surviving accounts in the San Francisco or Nevada press that indicate Twain was suffering from a venereal disease. However, syphilis is described by the medical profession as "the great imitator," because during its three distinct stages of progression its symptoms can resemble hundreds of other diseases.

The secondary stage of syphilis symptoms typically occur between six weeks and six months after the disease has been contracted, and consist of complaints such as headache, vague pains in bones and joints, and sore throat. Twain would report precisely these ailments during his Sandwich Islands sojourn, dismissing them in one case as "boo-hoo fever," a native virus, and otherwise ignoring them as unworthy of concern.

Until 1909, the year before Twain's death, there was no sure cure for syphilis. The cause of his demise was cardiovascular deficiency which led to a heart attack in his seventy-fifth year. Cardiovascular syphilis is one of the three symptomatic forms of the disease's late stages, often causing sudden, seemingly inexplicable death. The symptoms emulate exactly those of other cardiovascular disorders. If Twain had gone through life harboring a syphilitic infection, he may have believed it had "cured" itself after the first symptoms subsided, and gave it no further thought; he probably would have been unaware even at the end that his heart problems were due to the disease.

We will never know whether or not Twain actually had syphilis. If he did, he himself was probably unaware of it: the disease's early manifestations often go unnoticed or are misdiagnosed as other ailments, and in more than half of the cases of those who contract syphilis, the dreaded tertiary or final symptoms never appear. In a sense it is irrelevant whether or not he had the disease, for that cannot be determined. What is intriguing about the possibility of him having had a venereal disease is the fact that no mention of it has survived. Fitz Smythe could have been merely recording local scuttlebutt in his column; there was no pretense of cordiality in his rivalry with Twain. But while he was obviously flinging the worst mud he could find, he could also have been telling the truth. The researcher who digs up and pores over newspaper articles written by and about Twain during his Nevada and California days cannot fail to be fascinated by the picture of him that emerges; *that* Mark Twain was distinctly different from the fellow who would take up residency on the East Coast a few years later and proceed to become America's foremost literary figure. It is as if, after he left the West, an iron barrier had come clanging down, forever dividing the young man from the older one, and creating in place of the rakish, risk-taking young devil a more rational, moral, sedate citizen. Twain himself was undoubtedly the chief instigator of this biographical censorship; he was plainly uncomfortable with himself as the "Sage-brush Bohemian," or the author of "The Massacre at Dutch Nick's" and "Jim Smiley and His Jumping Frog." If he did have syphilis, he probably could never have admitted it, even to himself. It would have been an all-too-material relic of his wild days, better relegated to myth and rumor, best forgotten altogether like the raw and embarrassing life he had led in the West.

On March 7, 1866, Samuel Clemens hung over the rail of the *Ajax* as she steamed out of San Francisco harbor, leaning into the crisp, refreshing wind that whipped the wavelets of the Golden Gate into stiff white peaks and caused his bushy red hair to fly wildly about his face. The grimy, crowded streets clinging precariously to the steep hillsides of San Francisco receded into the distance as the steamer swung around the point, out of the bay, and into the open Pacific. Years later, after crisscrossing the globe dozens of times, Twain would be the most jaded and blasé of travelers, but in this spring of 1866 the mere notion that he was bound for unknown climes was enough to make him giddy with joy.

"We backed out from San Francisco at 4 P.M., all full—some full of tender regrets for severed associations, others full of buoyant anticipations of a pleasant voyage and a revivifying change of scene, and yet others full of schemes for extending their business relations and making larger profits. The balance were full of whiskey," he wrote in his first article for the Sacramento *Union*. He went on, "It was a pleasant, breezy afternoon, and the strange new sense of entire and perfect emancipation from labor and responsibility coming strong upon me, I went up on the hurricane deck so that I could have room to enjoy it. I sat down on a bench, and for an hour I took a tranquil delight in that kind of labor which is such a luxury to the enlightened Christian—to wit, the labor of other people. Captain Godfrey was 'making sail,' and he was moving the men around briskly."

Twain's "roving commission" for the *Union* was far from a plea-sure trip, however. His assignment was to write a daily letter for the next thirty days. Naively, he believed that the Sandwich (later the

Hawaiian) Islands would require only a month's visit for him to exhaust all the interesting facts, figures, and subject possibilities for articles. In fact, he would remain in the islands for four months and a day, and even then he wouldn't have covered everything of interest.

He wasted little time in getting down to work. He began canvassing the Sandwich Islands residents among the *Ajax*'s passengers, seeking information about the islands' geography and history. There was little else for him to do once the eleven-day voyage began to wear on his patience, for, as he wrote in his second *Union* article, "The most steady-going amusement the gentlemen had on the trip was euchre, and the most steady-going the ladies had was being seasick."

Just as he had used Clement Rice as "The Unreliable" to good advantage, Twain created "Mr. Brown," ostensibly his traveling companion during the Sandwich Islands jaunt, but in reality a catchall for every crude impulse Twain himself experienced and was ashamed to call his own. This bumpkin *doppelgänger* made his debut in Twain's first *Union* letter, and from then on his drunken, leering presence was constant in Twain's reports. Ignorant, colossally self-possessed, serenely and thoroughly profane—that was Brown. Early on, Twain struck on the inspired idea of having Brown read over his shoulder whenever he waxed especially poetic, and comment upon the proceedings with withering sarcasm, dashing the lofty expansiveness down to earth with a resounding thud. Brown was the original "Ugly American"—as, in some ways, was Twain himself.

Upon arrival in Honolulu at noon on March 18, Twain remained on board ship chatting with the crew for an hour or so while the other passengers debarked. He soon discovered that while he had tarried the passengers had taken all the lodging accommodations in town, forcing him to spend the night in his cabin on the *Ajax*. "It is very warm in the stateroom, no air enters the ports," he wrote in his first article. "Therefore, have dressed in a way which seems best calculated to suit the exigencies of the case. A description of this dress is not necessary. I may observe, however, that I bought the chief article of it at Ward's" (a men's clothing store in San Francisco that specialized in shirts and undergarments). He had come into the frontier in 1861 clad only in his underwear as his swaying stage-coach carried him westward across the Great American Desert; now he faced toward the horizon similarly unburdened with propriety.

His first impressions of Honolulu were of "Sunday stillness" (it *was* Sunday): "natives sitting in shade of houses on ground," as he recorded in his notebook. He proceeded down "long street darkest in the world, down to the Esplanade—width 3 buggies abreast" and into the distinctly non-Sabbath world of Nuuanu Street, downtown Honolulu's red-light district. The street was lined with cafes filled with "gaudy women" waiting to pick up well-heeled whalers. The air rang with the sounds of fandangos danced to violins, piano, and castanets. Twain presumably took a look and kept on going to record the fact that the "Hotels gouge Californians—charges sailing passengers eight dollars a week for board, but steamer passengers ten." But he went on to describe private Honolulu hospitality. "Richards said: 'Come in—sit down—take off your coat & boots—take a drink. Here is a pass-key to the liquor & cigar cupboard—put it in your pocket—two doors to this house—stand wide open night & day from January till January—no locks on them—march in whenever you feel like it, take as many drinks & cigars as you want, & make yourself at home." Another citizen reportedly told Twain, "Come in when you feel like it—take a drink, take a smoke—wash your feet in the water pitcher if you want to—wipe 'em on the bedclothes—break the furniture—spit on the table-cloth—throw the things out doors—make yourself comfortable—make yourself at home."

Twain's claim that he enjoyed "half a year's luxurious vagrancy in the islands" was one of his characteristic "stretchers": his visit lasted four months, and those months were not exactly frittered away in languorous idleness. During that period he would send back twenty-five articles to the *Union* which ranged in length from eighteen hundred to thirty-five hundred words. For each of these, he was paid twenty dollars—not a bad rate, until you consider how much hard work went into compiling the information that made up each article.

It didn't take long for Twain to realize that his initial thirty-day schedule was hopelessly optimistic. Political and economic conditions in the islands were fascinating, and transportation was primitive at best. Instead of succumbing to the islanders' hospitality, he got right to work, renting a horse from the livery stable at the American Hotel and setting off on a tour of the capital island, Oahu. This mount left a great deal to be desired, as "the first gate he came to he started in; I had neither whip nor spur, and so I simply argued the case with him," Twain wrote. "He firmly resisted argument, but ultimately yielded to insult and abuse . . . Within the next six hundred yards he crossed the street fourteen times and attempted thirteen gates, and in the meantime the tropical sun was beating down and threatening to cave the top of my head in, and I was literally dripping with perspiration and profanity. (I am only human and I was sorely aggravated. I shall behave better next time.)"

Christening the horse "Oahu" after the island (the animal was given to falling asleep on his feet when he wasn't trying to heave his rider off by lurching over six-foot stone walls), Twain passed through the "King's Grove" at Waikiki, an ancient stand of coconut trees where members of the Hawaiian royal family sometimes rested away from the rigors of court life. "The King's flag was flying from the roof of one of the cottages," he wrote, "and His Majesty was probably within. He owns the whole concern thereabouts, and passes his time there frequently, on sultry days 'laying off.' "

Just beyond the regal resort Twain found "an interesting ruin— the meager remains of an ancient heathen temple—a place where human sacrifices were offered up in those bygone days when the simple child of nature, yielding momentarily to sin when sorely tempted, acknowledged his error when calm reflection had shown it to him, and came forward with noble frankness and offered up his grandmother as an atoning sacrifice—in those old days when the luckless sinner could keep on cleansing his conscience and achieving periodic happiness as long as his relations held out."

Following his circuit of Oahu, Twain moved on to Maui, the next island in the chain, inspecting the burned-out volcanic crater of Haleakala, then riding up the lush Iao Valley. He subsequently traveled to the "big island" of Hawaii, where, among other things, he saw the volcano of Kilauea. Kilauea was still active during Twain's visit to the islands, and he had heard so much about it that he was determined to get as close to its explosive central crater as possible.

With an equally reckless fellow named Marlette acting as his guide, Twain walked directly across the floor of the volcano's crater by night, dashing lightly over sheets of fiery lava that flowed around his feet, and leaping across wide crevices from which the molten fire trapped inside emitted a baleful red glow.

At one point, Twain's guide suddenly shouted for him to stop. "I never stopped quicker in my life," Twain wrote in *Roughing It*. "I asked what the matter was. He said we were out of the path. He said we must not go on until we found it again, for we were surrounded with beds of rotten lava, through which we could easily break and plunge down 1,000 feet. I thought 800 would answer for me, and was about to say so, when Marlette partly proved his statement, crushing through and disappearing to his arm-pits."

Marlette managed to get out all right, and the two explorers proceeded to spend the rest of the night gazing down into the hellish depths of the red-hot crater. Twain remembered the experience vividly for the rest of his life, often retelling it in graphic terms that rendered visitors and acquaintances awe-struck.

The Kilauea adventure was a high point in his Sandwich Islands sojourn, and a welcome antidote to some of the more dismal aspects of his stay, such as traveling on interisland packets like the wretched *Boomerang*. The *Boomerang*'s route lay between Honolulu and the island of Hawaii, a trip of one hundred and fifty miles. She was a cramped, dingy, derelict craft with minuscule cabins for first-class passengers such as Twain. On the foredeck were "natives of both sexes, with their customary dogs, mats, blankets, pipes, calabashes of poi [a Hawaiian food made of fermented taro root], fleas, and other luxuries and baggage of minor importance. As soon as we set sail the natives all lay down on the deck as thick as Negroes in a slave pen, and smoked, conversed, and spit on each other, and were truly sociable."

The first night out, Twain recalled in *Roughing It*, he lay in his cabin, which was "rather larger than a hearse and dark as a vault. It had two coffins on each side—I mean two bunks." As he lay in his "coffin," watching the dim whale oil lantern swinging to the rolling of the ship, his olfactory senses lulled by the sweet scent of bilge water, he suddenly felt something gallop across him. He leaped to his feet, but climbed back into his bunk again when he discovered that it was merely a rat. Shortly thereafter he felt something else creeping across him. Thinking it might be a centipede, he got up once again. "The first glance at the pillow showed me a repulsive sentinel perched on each end of it—cockroaches as large as peach leaves—fellows with long, quivering antennae and fiery, malignant eyes. They were grating their teeth like tobacco worms, and appeared to be dissatisfied about something. I had often heard that these reptiles were in the habit of eating off sleeping sailors' toenails down to the quick, and I would not get in the bunk anymore. I lay down on the floor." But there was no peace anywhere. Soon came another rat, followed by a procession of cockroaches who set up camp in Twain's hair, and finally a troupe of acrobatic fleas who "were throwing double somersaults about my person in the wildest disorder, and taking a bite every time they struck."

Twain went on to conclude that this description was "not overdrawn; it is a truthful sketch of interisland schooner life. There is no such thing as keeping a vessel in elegant condition when she carries molasses and Kanakas."

But just as Twain had rarely complained about the bitter winter cold in Aurora, the dangers of lawless Virginia City, or any of the other physical and psychological hazards of frontier life, he endured rugged conditions such as those aboard the *Boomerang* without much comment. The novelty of island life was apparently enough to keep his mind off its discomforts.

He observed the islands' native population at some length and with the greatest of interest, just as he had surveyed local Indian tribes in California and Nevada. His was not the detached and analytical eye of the anthropologist, but the curious and eager one of the small-town boy peeping in under the sideshow tent. He had ultimately been able, in San Francisco, to appreciate the plight of the Chinese immigrant workers because they had a culture many thousands of years old, but he viewed the Kanakas as a race of savages, akin to the Paiutes or Goshoots of the Sierra Nevada region, blissfully ignorant of the morality or sense of purpose that he believed marked "civilized" races.

At noon one day on Kealakekua Bay, he observed a bevy of young nude native ladies disporting themselves near the water, and went down to look at them. "But with a prudery which seems to be characteristic of that sex everywhere, they all plunged in with a lying scream, and when they rose to the surface, they only just poked their heads out and showed no disposition to proceed any further in the same direction. I was naturally irritated by such conduct, and therefore I piled their clothes up on a boulder in the edge of the sea and sat down on them and kept the wenches in the water until they were pretty well used up. I had them in the door, as the missionaries say. I was comfortable, and I just let them beg . . . I finally gave it up and went away, hoping that the rebuke I had given them would not be lost upon them. I went and undressed and went in myself. And then they went out. I never saw such singular perversity."

He had found the Kanaka women attractive in an earlier letter, observing that "some of the younger women had very pretty faces and splendid black eyes and heavy masses of long black hair, occasionally put up in a 'net'; some of these dark, gingerbread colored beauties were on foot—generally on bare foot, I may add—and others were on horseback—astraddle; they never ride any other way, and they ought to know which way is best, for there are no more accomplished horsewomen in the world, it is said." But he was repulsed by their nonchalance when it came to sex, as evidenced by his reportage on the libidinous dance called the "hula hula," which he described, approvingly, as having been stopped by the missionaries acting in cahoots with the Hawaiian legislature, which the whites essentially dominated. And although he sent back a lengthy report on the funeral of Princess Victoria Kaahumanu Kamamalu, who had died at the age of twenty-seven, he made no mention of the cause of death. That fact he reserved for a succinct and withering note in his personal notebook: "[Princess Victoria] died in forcing abortion—kept half a dozen bucks to do her washing, & has suffered 7 abortions." Much later in his life he still appeared to be queasy about the subject, writing in his *Autobiography*: "In the Sandwich Islands in 1866 a buxom royal princess died. Occupying a place of distinguished honor at her funeral were thirty-six splendidly built young native men. In a laudatory song which celebrated the various merits, achievements and accomplishments of the late princess those thirty-six stallions were called her *harem*, and the song said it had been her pride and boast that she kept the whole of them busy, and that several times it had happened that more than one of them had been able to charge overtime."

His assessment of the natives was that sexual excess, cannibalism, and pagan religious beliefs made their conversion by Christian missionaries not only desirable, but absolutely necessary. Whenever he had an opportunity he inserted words of praise for the Protestant missionaries into his *Union* articles, just as whenever he described native customs and history he fell back on clichés about ignorance, nakedness, barbarism, and so on. His description of the president of the Hawaiian Assembly, His Royal Highness M. Kekuanoa, is indicative of his attitude.

The President is the King's father. He is an erect, strongly built, massive featured, white haired, swarthy old gentleman of eighty years of age or thereabouts. He was simply but well dressed, in a blue cloth coat and white vest, and white pantaloons, without spot, dust, or blemish upon them. He bears himself with a calm, stately dignity, and is a man of noble presence. He was a young man and a distinguished warrior under that terrific old fighter, Kamehameha I, more than half a century ago, and I could not help saying to myself, "This man, naked as the day he was born, and war club and spear in hand, has charged at the head of a horde of savages against other hordes of savages far back in the past, and reveled in slaughter and carnage; has worshiped wooden images on his bended knees; has seen hundreds of his race offered up in heathen temples as sacrifices to hideous idols, at a time when no missionary's foot had ever pressed this soil; and he had never heard of the white man's God; has believed his enemy could secretly pray him to death; has seen the day, in his childhood, when it was a crime punishable by death for a man to eat with his wife, or for a plebeian to let his shadow fall upon the King—and now look at him: an educated Christian; neatly and handsomely dressed; a high-minded, elegant gentleman; a traveler, in some degree, and one who has been the honored guest of royalty in Europe; a man practiced in holding the reins of an enlightened government, and well versed in the politics of his country and, in general, practical information. Look at him, sitting there presiding over the deliberations of a legislative body, among whom are white men—a grave, dignified, statesmanlike personage, and as seemingly natural and fitted to the place as if he had been born in it and had never been out of it in his lifetime. Lord! how the experiences of this old man's strange, eventful life must shame the cheap inventions of romance!"

The generally sagacious Twain did not even seem to grasp the fact that, by 1866, the missionaries' influence on the islands was definitely on the wane; their heyday had been in the two previous decades, and although some of the more prominent Protestants had entrenched themselves firmly in Hawaiian government and enterprise, changing conditions in the islands were rapidly rendering their presence superfluous.

The proprietors of the *Union* had agreed to send Twain to the islands because of those changing conditions. The Sandwich Islands were beginning to realize their economic dependence upon the United States as a market for their sugar, rice, and cotton industries. In the early years of the nineteenth century the islands had enjoyed a financial bonanza from the multitude of whalers passing through the region, but whaling had begun to peter out in the early 1860s, the victim of a diminishing whale population, an increasing petroleum industry, and the sabotage of whaling ships by Confederate privateers. It was apparent to clear-thinking Sandwich Islands businessmen that the old days of insularity and self-complacency were gone forever. On the other side of the Pacific, California capitalists were beginning to be curious about these paradisiacal islands, with their yearlong growing season. Mark Twain, one of the West Coast's most popular writers, could do a great deal to bridge the gap between potential investors and eager planters.

And thump the drum he did. In article after article he sang the praises of the sugar industry, the rice industry, and the coffee plantations on the Kona Coast. He rhapsodized about the easy availability of reliable "coolie labor," which would make the harvesting of Hawaiian crops cheap and profitable for American investors. He even went so far as to champion the cause of annexing the islands to the United States. He had been given an assignment, and he made sure to fulfill it to the letter.

Twain soon discovered that his reputation as the most popular writer on the Pacific Coast had preceded him to the islands. As the center of attention wherever he went, he seemed to enjoy playing up to his reputation as the wild man from the Washoe wilderness, dressing in a linen duster and exhibiting exaggerated personal mannerisms. He gave a rather cartoonish account of his effect on the populace in one of his *Union* letters, describing how, while riding back from a visit to an old heathen graveyard, he and his companion "Brown" had become separated from the rest of their party. Stopping in front of a private residence to wait for them, Twain "soon saw that I had attracted the attention of a comely young girl, and I felt duly flattered. Perhaps, thought I, she admires my horsemanship—and I made a savage jerk at the bridle and said, 'Ho! will you!' to show how fierce and unmanageable the beast was—though, to say truly, he was leaning up against a hitching post peaceably enough at the time. . . ." He galloped around on his horse for her benefit, meanwhile pretending he was unconscious of her attentions. "I then addressed a few 'peart' remarks to Brown, to give the young lady a chance to admire my style of conversation, and was gratified to see her step up and whisper to Brown and glance furtively at me at the same time . . . As soon as we started home, I asked with a fair show of indifference what she had been saying."

Brown laughed and said, " 'She thought from the slouchy way you rode and the way you drawled out your words, that you was drunk! She said, "Why don't you take the poor creature home, Mr. Brown? It makes me nervous to see him galloping that horse and just hanging on that way, and he so drunk." ' "

At the end of June he returned to Honolulu from his wanderings, intending to lay up for a while and nurse the saddle boils he had accumulated during his travels on horseback around the islands. He was lying in bed in his room at the American Hotel when he received a message from some very august personages indeed, saying that they were going to call on him at his hotel the next morning.

This was a summons no man could refuse, for the party was headed up by His Excellency Anson Burlingame, who had just arrived on the *Ajax* from San Francisco en route to a diplomatic post as American minister to China. He was accompanied by some other Americans who were traveling to China with him—Generals Van Valkenberg and Rumsey, and Burlingame's eighteen-year-old son, Edward. Twain was no stranger to the workings of politics, nor was he particularly sentimental when it came to the bloated aristocrats of political pomp. Nonetheless, after hearing through channels in Honolulu that Edward Burlingame was a big fan of "Jumping Frog" and wanted very much to meet its author, he determined to mingle with the group. However, he realized that it would be quite unseemly, saddle boils or no saddle boils, to oblige such an exalted committee to wait upon him in his hotel room, so the next morning he dragged himself painfully out of bed, applied a pair of pants as gingerly as he could over the affected area, and drove with all haste to the house belonging to the American minister to the Sandwich Islands, where Burlingame and company were quartered.

His visit was an unqualified success, for he took care to pull out all the stops and make himself thoroughly agreeable and amusing. The diplomats found his charm irresistible. For his part, Twain was considerably impressed by Anson Burlingame, and remained so throughout his life. During their conversation, Burlingame gave him a piece of advice that in some ways echoed that of Artemus Ward: "You have great ability; I believe you have genius. What you need now is refinement of association. Seek companionship among men of superior intellect and character. Refine yourself and your work. Never affiliate with inferiors; always climb."

Twain took this advice very much to heart—for better or for worse. It was consistent with his own philosophy, for one thing; despite his reporter's cynicism toward politicians, paradoxically he also had always had a weak spot for men like Burlingame, with their public heroics and reflected glory. Always seeking the approval of role models, he had sought out Bret Harte and Artemus Ward in similar fashion, and he would likewise work hard, a few years later in New England, to cultivate friendships with people he felt he should be associated with. There was an ironic element to Twain's social climbing—his willingness to chase after the big names of the moment probably contributed materially to his success as a writer, which enabled him to develop his genius publicly rather than languishing in obscurity, the way a more modest person would have. Had he not possessed this instinct, he may very well have remained a regional humorist whose reputation died with him. And yet his panting after essentially no-account figures, whom he took at face value, was something he would come to rue in his later years.

Anson Burlingame was a former Massachusetts state legislator and failed minister to Austria whose chief accomplishment was helping to open up China to Western imperialism. Although he was extremely celebrated during his lifetime, a period during which the American public shared Twain's love of ringing oratory and handsome uniforms, Burlingame was a shrewd politician rather than a man of vision. His geniality and easy conversation, coupled with the yards of gold braid and dazzling metal on the uniforms of Van Valkenberg and Rumsey, dazzled Twain.

Burlingame did Twain a tangible favor, however, by helping him get a "scoop" on a very important story. A large steamship, the *Hornet*, had left New York some weeks earlier and had caught fire in the middle of the ocean, leaving fifteen survivors to battle the rolling deep for forty-five days in a tiny lifeboat with only ten days' rations of food and water. Eleven of these miserable skeletons had arrived in Honolulu on June 21, and Twain instantly determined to interview the sufferers for national papers. He was the only correspondent for any American paper then in the islands. The problem was, his exertions during the past three months had left him feeble and exhausted, and he was under doctors' orders to get in bed and stay there. How, then, could he drag himself to the hospital in Honolulu where the survivors were, and interview them?

It was Anson Burlingame to the rescue. Burlingame, with military decisiveness, ascertained the situation at once, and without further ado bore the prostrate Twain to the hospital on a stretcher, then proceeded to interview the survivors himself while Twain propped himself up on his elbow and took notes. That night he wrote feverishly and finished his article just in time to heave it aboard the California-bound steamer as it was leaving Honolulu pier the next morning. The scoop on the *Hornet* disaster ran in three columns on the front page of the *Union*, and was the first and fullest story of the tragedy to appear in any American newspaper.

By early July, Twain had fully recovered, and he boarded ship for San Francisco on July 19 on the vessel *Smyrniote*. He spent most of the voyage home talking with the captain of the ill-fated *Hornet*, as well as with some of the other survivors, who were headed for San Francisco. He also copied passages from their assorted diaries. It was his intention to write an article about the disaster for a New York magazine—thinking, no doubt, of the further inroads this might make into the East Coast literary enclave.

During the voyage home he otherwise employed himself by leading the ship's choir during Sunday services. Aboard the *Smyrniote* was the Reverend Franklin S. Rising, with whom Twain had been close when Rising was rector of Virginia City's Episcopal church. "I hope they will have a better opinion of our music in heaven than I have down here," he reflected in his journal. "If they don't a thunderbolt will knock this vessel endways." The heavens did make a sort of gesture in his direction, however; on the night of July 27 he saw a moonlit rainbow, but he looked upon it as representing an auspicious omen.

In his notebook he also scribbled brief entries which would appear in *Huckleberry Finn* some years later—memories of childhood superstitions—and a line, "Cat & painkiller," which would find its way into *Tom Sawyer*.

However, once he arrived in San Francisco and was faced immediately with the same old grind he thought he had left behind, he was afflicted with the remorse that affects every traveler on returning home. "God help me, I wish I were at sea again!" he confided to his journal.

In Sacramento, the last of his Sandwich Islands articles were running in the *Union* and were being very well received by the public. Twain accordingly made another trip to the "City of Saloons" to report for the *Union* on the California State Fair—or rather, on the horse races that were one of the fair's biggest attractions. He may have done so as a favor to the *Union*'s James Anthony, for it was rather routine work and in some ways even reminiscent of the ignominious drudgery he had suffered as the *Call*'s lokulitems. But the favor ultimately paid off handsomely, if in a roundabout way, for when the time came for the settling of accounts between Twain and Anthony for the *Hornet* disaster scoop, the *Union*'s proprietor was extremely generous. "How much do you think it ought to be, Mark?" Anthony asked Twain.

"Oh, I'm a modest man; I don't want the whole *Union* office," replied Twain with mock diffidence. "Call it $100 a column."

Anthony and Paul Morrill laughed, but they made out a payment order for the amount Twain specified. Twain took it down to the paper's cashier, who could only stare apoplectically at the amount. "He didn't faint," Twain remembered in *Roughing It*, "but he came rather near it. He sent for the proprietors, and they only laughed, in their jolly fashion, and said it was a robbery, but 'no matter, pay it.'" It was little wonder that Twain recalled them fondly as "the best men that ever owned a newspaper."

9

The Trouble Begins at Eight

Back in San Francisco, the enervated Twain was forced back into the grim reality of earning a living. After the luxurious greenery of the Sandwich Islands, San Francisco seemed barren and dreary to him. "San Francisco, a truly fascinating city to live in, is stately and handsome at a fair distance, but close at hand one notes that the architecture is mostly old-fashioned, many streets are made up of decaying, smoke-grimed, wooden houses, and the barren sand-hills towards the outskirts obtrude themselves too prominently." This was how he later described the city in *Roughing It*, and it is a fair assumption that the description also reflected his feelings about San Francisco at the time he returned from the islands.

Despite his popularity as a humorous journalist, he was feeling impatient about his career. Although "Jumping Frog" had earned a sort of celebrity on both coasts, he didn't seem to have set his feet on any sure path to continuing literary success. He had had high hopes for his article on the *Hornet* disaster, which had been accepted and published by *Harper's* magazine in New York, but much to his dismay, the piece had run under the byline "Mark Swain" thanks to some careless typesetter. It was one of the maddening occurrences that were to make such great material for his subsequent books and essays, but at the moment it happened he felt far from philosophical about it.

Despite his depression at being back in the grimy city and forced once again to scramble for his bread and butter, Twain was formulating—as usual—all sorts of plans for future projects. He had an idea for a series of articles in *Harper's*, or any national magazine, which would enlarge on his *Union* letters from the Sandwich Islands. Such a series, he reasoned, could prove popular enough in the long run to enable him to wangle a book contract to further expand the articles. Travel books were extremely welcome to readers in an age when the only long-distance travel was accomplished by the slow and costly steamboat. As a matter of fact, Twain himself was, like his contemporaries, an inveterate reader of travel books. He had turned to them for facts and figures while writing his Sandwich Islands articles—sometimes poking fun at or otherwise castigating their authors in the course of his writing—but he also enjoyed perusing them for sheer entertainment. He was well aware of the marketability of such books, for he knew a number of California-based authors who in essence were being paid to travel; that is, they received sizable sums for books about their peregrinations. One of these authors was J. Ross Browne, a personal friend of Twain's whose travel books had enabled him to build a sumptuous and exotic home in Berkeley, where Twain sometimes stayed. After Twain had achieved national fame, Browne would jocularly accuse him of "borrowing" from his travel books, an accusation which could have come from dozens of travel writers, living and dead—and not only in Twain's case. Most travel writers "cribbed" copiously from guidebooks and histories, relying on them for facts and figures to buttress their own observations. There was generally a thin line between research and plagiarism, one made even blurrier by constant traffic.

Another lucrative calling for professional travel writers was the public lecture. Travel lectures were even more popular than travel books and could bring in considerable revenue for those with the nerve and stamina to undertake lecturing tours. In view of his literary reputation in the West, Twain felt he would have no trouble filling halls in San Francisco, Sacramento, Washoe, and the California mining towns. But he hesitated. It was one thing to entertain the members of the Third House with pseudo-political bombast, or to amuse Bret Harte with Mother Lode yarns. But delivering an informative lecture to a stiff and starchy audience who had paid for the privilege of hearing him—that was something entirely different.

Like the former steamboat pilot he was, Twain decided to "test the water" before attempting to navigate in it. He wrote out a rough draft of his proposed Sandwich Islands lecture and showed it to some friends whose opinions he valued. Unfortunately, he didn't receive much encouragement. A reporter he knew, for instance, looked over the lecture and expressed the fear that Twain might not be able to talk as well as he could write. Bret Harte and Charles Stoddard, whose opinions Twain practically took for gospel in those days, tendered similar doubts. It was only when Colonel John McComb of the *Alta California* read Twain's proposed lecture, wrung Twain's hand with vigor, and bellowed, "Do it, by all means! It will be a grand success, I know it! Take the largest house in town, and charge a dollar a ticket!" that the fledgling lecturer felt somewhat encouraged.

He also felt slightly ill at the thought of asking people to pay so bloated and grandiose a sum merely to hear him drawl his way through descriptions of heathens and volcanoes. Still, charging a dollar a ticket was so audacious that it was bound to attract a considerable number of curiosity seekers. So he proceeded over to Maguire's Opera House on Pine Street, the newest and fanciest theater in San Francisco. Tom Maguire, its proprietor, had owned the opera house in Virginia City and was an old acquaintance of Twain's, and he agreed to let the aspiring lecturer have his establishment for half the usual rate—only fifty dollars a night.

On September 27, 1866, the people of San Francisco discovered that the city had been liberally plastered with the following announcement:

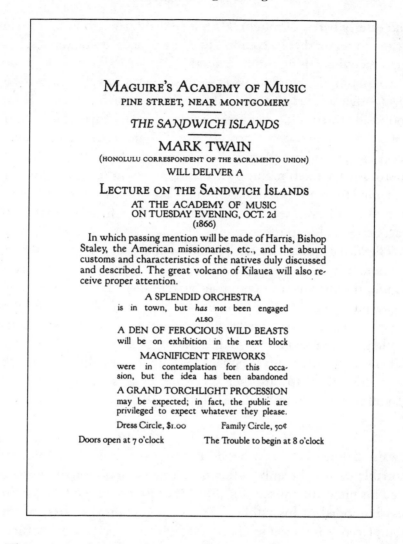

MAGUIRE'S ACADEMY OF MUSIC
PINE STREET, NEAR MONTGOMERY

THE SANDWICH ISLANDS

MARK TWAIN
(HONOLULU CORRESPONDENT OF THE SACRAMENTO UNION)
WILL DELIVER A

LECTURE ON THE SANDWICH ISLANDS
AT THE ACADEMY OF MUSIC
ON TUESDAY EVENING, OCT. 2d
(1866)

In which passing mention will be made of Harris, Bishop Staley, the American missionaries, etc., and the absurd customs and characteristics of the natives duly discussed and described. The great volcano of Kilauea will also receive proper attention.

A SPLENDID ORCHESTRA
is in town, but *has not* been engaged
ALSO
A DEN OF FEROCIOUS WILD BEASTS
will be on exhibition in the next block

MAGNIFICENT FIREWORKS
were in contemplation for this occasion, but the idea has been abandoned

A GRAND TORCHLIGHT PROCESSION
may be expected; in fact, the public are privileged to expect whatever they please.

Dress Circle, $1.00   Family Circle, 50¢

Doors open at 7 o'clock   The Trouble to begin at 8 o'clock

This same advertisement assaulted the eyes of San Francisco's citizens from the pages of several newspapers. Like the bogus "Duke" in *Huckleberry Finn*, Twain, a devoted frequenter of minstrel and burlesque shows, knew enough about lurid advertising to understand what would "fetch them."

Now, however, he proceeded to sweat. First he looked over his lecture notes in the cold, harsh light of reality, and it seemed to him that nothing he had ever clapped eyes on was as tiresome, tedious, and utterly bereft of humor. He felt so disheartened, in fact, that he began to regret that he couldn't just "bring a coffin on the stage and turn the whole thing into a funeral."

Expecting the absolute worst—or so he later explained in *Roughing It*—he decided to stagger his odds as best he could. He buttonholed three old drinking companions—"giants in stature, cordial by nature, and stormy-voiced"—and asked if they would serve as "plants" in the audience on the fateful (or, Twain projected morosely, the fatal) night. "This thing is going to be a failure," he observed to them melodramatically. "The jokes in it are so dim that nobody will ever see them; I would like to have you sit in the parquette, and help me through."

The three good fellows agreed wholeheartedly to laugh uproariously at even the most slender excuse for a joke. Next Twain sought out the wife of "a popular citizen"—actually, Mrs. Low, the Governor's wife—and explained to her, as he had to his three friends, that he feared his lecture was going to need all the help it could get. He asked if she would sit in the box to the left of the stage. Whenever he threw out the punch line of an especially obscure joke, he would turn toward her and smile, as a signal. Then she "shouldn't wait to investigate—but *respond*!"

Twain claimed later that he ate nothing for three days before the horrible event—he only suffered. While he undoubtedly exaggerated his prelecture misery for the sake of literature, he was nonetheless reminded of his public folly as the day drew nearer, making complacency impossible. The *Alta*, which served as the "official" lecture organ, ran bulletins on the impending event, declaring that Twain's friend Mr. Brown would "sing a refrain in the Kanaka tongue" and promising that the lecture would be "high-toned"— provided the orator spoke loudly enough. Other papers, in less absurd terms, predicted that the lecture would be a big success, and essentially ensured that it would be by exhorting their readers to show up early to get tickets "as there is every indication of a grand rush."

Nonetheless, in *Roughing It* Twain painted a spectacularly gloomy and devastating picture. At four in the afternoon on the day of the lecture, he claimed, he crept down to the box office at Maguire's; that was the time when the tickets for the evening's performance went on sale. Much to his horror, he found that the ticket office was locked up and the ticket seller had gone home. "No sales," he said to himself, and added bitterly, "I might have known it!" Desperately, he contemplated an array of last-minute ruses and dodges to get him out of the public humiliation he was sure the lecture would be—everything from faked illness to ignominious flight to a reprise of "pistols or poison, exit *me*"—but, ironically, lacked the courage to go through with them.

At six that evening, he approached Maguire's by way of the back alley and sneaked in through the stage door. The auditorium was empty, dark, resoundingly silent. For a brief moment he stood on the stage, staring dully out at the rows upon rows of empty seats. He turned, finally, and went back into the wings, where for an hour and a half he gave himself up to "the horrors," wholly unconscious of everything else.

"Then," he recalled in *Roughing It*, "I heard a murmur. It rose higher and higher, and ended in a crash, mingled with cheers . . . There was a pause, and then another; presently came a third, and before I well knew what I was about, I was in the middle of the stage, staring at a sea of faces, bewildered by the fierce glare of the lights, and quaking in every limb with a terror that seemed like to take my life away. The house was full, aisles and all!"

The trouble, as he had promised, had begun at eight.

Twain's version of that first lecture, full as it is of the mingled sense of drama and absurdity that characterize his style of narration, has more than one gaping hole in it. He certainly never believed that his lecture would fail to draw a crowd; his reputation as one of the West's most popular writers, not to mention the recent fame of "Jumping Frog," was sure to pull in a capacity audience. And even if he had been a virtual nonentity, the zealous P. T. Barnum missionary work of San Francisco's newspapers would have procured an audience for him. In retrospect it is not so hard to take Twain's version of

141

his first lecture at face value, for there is something undeniably noble about the notion of triumph snatched from the jaws of oblivion; but in truth, the estimated house count that night numbered between fifteen hundred and two thousand fashionably dressed, socially prominent San Franciscans. Maguire's Opera House was literally packed to the rafters, with a large number of male attendees being forced to stand against the wall in back.

That night, Twain opened his remarks with an eloquent apology for the absence of the orchestra he had promised in his advertisements. He explained that he had gone so far as to hire the services of "a performer on a gorgeous trombone," but had discovered that that unreasonable individual had required half a dozen other musicians to "help him." Since he had hired the trombonist to *work*, Twain told the audience, he had been obliged to let the fellow go promptly upon hearing such nonsense.

This was met with peals of laughter from the audience. Twain proceeded to unravel a string of other jokes, and finally, judging that the climate was appropriate, he commenced the weighty part of the lecture—the portion pertaining to the Sandwich Islands. He delineated the virtues of the Kanakas at some length, and touched on their vices with good-natured humor. He gave pertinent data on the islands' climate, vegetation, government, history, traditions, superstitions, religion, politics, government, royalty, manners, and customs—all of which weighty material was presented in painless fashion. During the course of the lecture, he also recommended that the United States annex the islands to the mainland, and enthused about the economic advantages the islands would offer, once they were under the protection of the U.S. (This gung-ho imperialism, apparently heartfelt, was due to give way to a more enlightened philosophical policy, until finally he would be able to state, some years later, that he was "opposed to having the eagle put its talons on any other land.")

As he had in his *Union* articles, Twain let the missionaries off rather lightly during the lecture, praising them for having rid the Kanakas of superstition and elevated the natives to a peaceful, if still largely uncivilized, condition. Most of the members of the audience

SEVERE CASE OF STAGE-FRIGHT.

knew that Twain occasionally attended San Francisco's Presbyterian church (he never missed an opportunity to inform his readers when he did, or of the fact that some of his best friends were ministers). No doubt his pious propaganda was sincere, although he would eventually begin billing his Sandwich Islands lecture as "Our Fellow Savages of the Sandwich Islands."

The high point of the evening was Twain's lofty and eloquent description of Mt. Kilauea, a description that reportedly had the audience's more susceptible members dabbing at their eyes with their handkerchiefs. In his characteristic drawl, Twain let roll off his tongue the most vivid description of an erupting volcano that had ever roused an audience to a standing ovation. "When the volcano of Kilauea broke through, a few years ago, lava flowed out of it for twenty days and twenty nights, and made a stream forty miles in length, until it reached the sea, tearing up forests in its awful fiery path, swallowing up huts, destroying all vegetation, rioting through shady dells and sinuous canyons. Amid this carnival of destruction, majestic columns of smoke ascended and formed a cloudy, murky pall overhead. Sheets of green, blue, lambent flames were shot upward, and pierced the vast gloom, making all sublimely grand."

At the end of this speech, he looked out at the audience to gauge its reaction, and his eye inadvertently caught that of Mrs. Governor Low. His conversation with her flashed into his mind, causing him to smile in spite of himself, whereupon she promptly took it for her signal to turn on the "laugh track." She broke into a mellow chuckle which rapidly infected the rest of the audience, obliterating Twain's "poor morsel of pathos." But he let it go; he knew the evening had been an unalloyed success.

When Twain finally concluded his lecture, which lasted an hour and a half (an unheard-of length for such an event), the audience simply refused to let him off the stage. He excused himself and walked off into the wings, but the crowd stood up and persistently applauded, cheered, and stamped until it seemed as though the roof would cave in. At this unanimous command, Twain shuffled back onstage again, looking around with a puzzled expression as if he couldn't understand what all the commotion was about. Then, pressed by the audience to say something further, he apologized to everyone for having "inflicted" his lecture on them in the first place. He explained that he was writing a book about the islands and said that he needed money to get it published. After receiving another thunderous round of applause that seemed to rival an erupting Kilauea for sheer number of decibels, Twain bowed once again and left the stage while the audience continued to applaud, stamp, and holler.

The next day all the San Francisco papers were full of Twain's triumph. The *Evening Bulletin* trumpeted that "as a humorous writer Mark Twain stands in the foremost rank, while his effort of last evening affords reason for the belief that he can establish an equal reputation as a humorous and original lecturer." The *Dramatic Chronicle* declared that his lecture "may be pronounced one of the greatest successes of the season."

Only Twain's former fellow *Golden Era* scribe, Prentice Mulford, felt obliged to be a little contrary. Mulford had, among other things, taken a largely unsuccessful crack at public lecturing in California's mining towns, and he now warned Twain about attempting a lecture career. "I shall venture on the terrible task of criticizing Mark Twain," he said. "It is a perilous undertaking. He wields a pen mightily in ridicule and sarcasm, and woe unto him who provokes his displeasure." Mulford went on to tease Twain gently. "Indeed it is not right that in one person should be combined so many species of talent. It is enough that [Twain] is a good writer. Let the gifts be distributed equally." Like some of the other reviewers, Mulford noted that Twain's speaking voice could have been louder at times, a fault evidenced by many new to the lecture platform. Mulford concluded his review by cautioning Twain on the many pitfalls that awaited a lecturer touring mining camps and other outposts of civilization.

All those who reviewed the lecture were unanimous on one point: as a lecturer, Twain was far superior to his old friend and mentor Artemus Ward. Mulford pointed out, "Mark's humor is his own, while much of Ward's is begged and borrowed." Twain had certainly paid close attention to Ward's platform mannerisms, and while no one could accuse him of actually stealing from Ward, it was plain that he had made many valuable mental notes about what went over well with Ward's audiences. But there all similarities ended, for where Ward relied heavily upon tricks and showmanship to put his lectures over, Twain's success relied upon his verbal prowess and his own powerful personality.

It was obvious to everyone that Twain's personal style had contributed vitally to the remarkable success of his first lecture. With considerable shrewdness, he had played up his lack of experience as a public lecturer. He had approached the podium looking down at the floor and virtually radiating nervousness (this wasn't entirely for dramatic effect—he later admitted to being so terrified with stage fright for a few minutes that he got it all out of his system and was never troubled by it again), and began to speak hesitantly. During the lecture, his face had worn an anxious, worried expression; his delivery was framed in his own inimitable drawl, with the words coming so slowly that one Washoe newspaper compositor was later to observe that it sounded as though there was "a three-em quad" (in typesetting, a wide space) between each one. Then, too, the audience could instantly empathize when Twain seemed to appear thunderstruck every time he scored a humorous hit with the audience, as though he couldn't believe his own success.

Most unusually for a lecturer at that time, Twain eschewed the customary pompous oratory in favor of a strictly conversational delivery. He used the same approach in his writing, but since he wrote primarily for newspapers at this point in his career, his colloquial approach in that medium was far less noticeable. The critics were sharply divided when it came to his penchant for lacing his lecture with liberal doses of slang. Bret Harte, always mindful of the proprieties, complained that Twain's faults as a lecturer were "crudeness, coarseness and an occasional Panurge-like plainness of statement." But Harte praised Twain for exhibiting "the Western character of ludicrous exaggeration and audacious statement," which, he felt, was even more indicative of the national American character than the Yankee platform delineations of New England writer James Russell Lowell.

Nonetheless, none of the writers who reviewed Twain's first public lecture really hit on the fundamental reason for his success, both in writing and in public speaking. This was simply that Twain was able to communicate a basically human quality that few people could resist. At the root of his humor was a thorough understanding of human folly, his own and other people's, with all its capacity for self-delusion, arrogance, folly—and nobility. It was easy for Twain's audience to identify with him when he stood, shaking in his shoes, behind the lectern; their hearts went out to him as he sweated and drawled his way through what was actually an extremely eloquent speech. Perhaps this wasn't the first time anyone had combined pathos and humor with eloquence, but when Twain did so, any previous practitioners of that art were instantly forgotten. It was a tribute to his own originality and daring that the lecture had gone so well; but the cordial Western audience at Maguire's Opera House had helped some too. If their reception of that first lecture hadn't been so enthusiastic, Twain would never have been launched on the platform career that was to last for the rest of his life, enabling him, as he later said, never to have to work for a living again.

When Twain counted up the proceeds from his lecture, he was no doubt impressed with his own business acumen. The gross came to twelve hundred dollars; after paying for the advertising and giving Tom Maguire fifty dollars for the rental of the Opera House, Twain still had four hundred dollars left in his pocket.

As news of the first lecture began to spread via newspapers all over the Pacific Coast and Nevada, the most logical thing seemed to be for Twain to undertake a lecture tour of California and Nevada. He had probably decided to lecture in Sacramento, Virginia City, and Carson City even before he appeared in San Francisco, and since the reviews had been uniformly good, he now added additional dates in Marysville, Grass Valley, Nevada City, Red Dog, You Bet, Gold Hill, Silver City, Dayton, and Washoe.

With the itinerary set, the next step was to appoint a business manager. He chose Denis McCarthy, the same fellow who had been sitting in the office of the *Enterprise* on the day back in 1862 when the dusty and demented Samuel Clemens had wandered in from his 130-mile hike across the Washoe wasteland. This fact alone endeared McCarthy to Twain; besides, McCarthy had been one of his boon companions during drinking sprees and other recreations, and had masterfully assisted Twain, Dan De Quille, and Joe Goodman during Artemus Ward's riotous stay in Virginia City. Such abilities would come in handy on the lecture tour.

The first leg of the trip, from San Francisco to Sacramento, was made aboard the Sacramento steamship, Twain's favorite means of transportation to the state capital—there were rail connections, but only steamboats had saloon facilities. In Sacramento, Twain and McCarthy dreamed up a sensation-laden publicity campaign. Posters announcing Twain's Sandwich Islands lecture advised potential attendees that Twain would dispense his wisdom from the lecture platform for one night only . . . and for only a portion of that night. The puffery went on: "THE CELEBRATED BEARDED WOMAN! Is not with this Circus. THE WONDERFUL COW WITH SIX LEGS! Is not attached to this Menagerie. That Curious and Unaccountable Freak of Nature, THE IRISH GIANT! Who stands 9 feet 6 inches in height and has a breadth of beam in proportion . . . will not be present and need not be expected. THE KING OF THE ISLANDS! failed to arrive in season for the Lecture in San Francisco, but may confidently be expected on this Occasion." As before, the orgies were to commence at eight.

The Sacramento lecture went off as well as the one in San Francisco had, with a capacity house and favorable notices in the Sacramento *Union* and *Bee.* After the lecture, Twain paid a visit to his friends Anthony and Morrill at the *Union*, this time trying to convince them to send him on an all-expenses-paid trip around the world in exchange for a further series of travel letters. However, Anthony and Morrill kept their purse strings closed this time, preferring to see Twain's lecturing career pursued and their own solvency maintained a while longer.

Leaving the "City of Saloons," Twain and McCarthy headed for the mining towns of the western Sierra Nevada, with Marysville their first stop. At their next stop, in Grass Valley, Twain and McCarthy were approached by a former *Enterprise* compositor whose wife had a tightrope-walking act. She was scheduled to stage a performance in Grass Valley on the night that Twain had planned to lecture there. Her husband suggested that Twain combine his lecturing performance with that of the acrobat, after a fashion—he proposed that his wife string up her wire outside the hall where Twain was to speak, since the crowd she drew would then have a tendency to drift into the auditorium to hear Twain's lecture. But Twain refused, claiming later that he had never liked the man.

Also in Grass Valley, Twain carried his flamboyant advertising one step further. In the poster for his lecture he declared that after the lecture was over he would perform a series of "wonderful feats of SLEIGHT OF HAND, if desired to do so." At a given signal, he promised, he would go out with any gentleman member of the audience and take a drink. Also, if the public wished, he would "repeat this unique and interesting feat" until the audience was firmly convinced that this was no act of bogus legerdemain. Furthermore, the poster declared, Twain would, at a moment's warning, leave town without paying his hotel bill. He claimed that he had previously performed this trick on many other occasions, both in San Francisco and elsewhere, and that it had always been received with enthusiastic comment—although he neglected to say from whom these comments issued. Finally, he advertised, "at any hour of the night, after 10," he would "go through any house in the city, no matter how dark it may be, and take an inventory of its contents, and not miss as many of the articles as the owner will in the morning."

During that first lecture tour, Twain found himself speaking before patrician listeners in opera houses with red velvet drop curtains and bright footlights, and also before audiences of rusty sourdoughs in mining camp "academies" with only a row of smoking tallow candles or kerosene lanterns to separate him from his hearers. Wherever he spoke, he always came on stage carrying his lecture notes rolled up under his arm. These notes had been printed on brown wrapping paper in very large letters so that he could make them out under adverse lighting conditions. The sheets of wrapping paper were generally out of order, and Twain got a great deal of humorous mileage out of shuffling them flamboyantly until they were even more hopelessly mixed and the audience was in convulsions.

One of Denis McCarthy's most important functions as tour manager was to secure, in each town, a person to introduce the speaker. This convention was widespread at that time, and it would have been unthinkable for Twain not to have someone introduce him before he began to speak. Later, he would assume this office himself, stating that he was as capable of anyone else of enumerating his own virtues, but during his first lecture tour he did not attempt to break with tradition. Eleventh-hour scrambles for an announcer led to many totally unforeseen introductions. In Red Dog, a tiny mining camp on the Stanislaus River, an introducer had been selected prior to the lecture, but he failed to show up at the appointed time.

McCarthy was obliged to scan the audience desperately for a last-minute stand-in, suitable or otherwise. Finally he plucked an old miner out of the assemblage, a reluctant geezer who tried to slip out of McCarthy's iron grip, but failed. He was half-dragged, half-carried to the platform, where he cleared his throat, glanced around wildly, and said, "Ladies and gentlemen, this here is the celebrated Mark Twain from the celebrated city of San Francisco, with his celebrated lecture about the celebrated Sandwich Islands." Twain rarely had an introduction as ludicrous as that one, unless you counted the time in another California mining town when a grizzled forty-niner with apparently no taste for puffery grumbled, "Ladies and gentlemen, I know only two things about this man; the first is that he's never been in jail, and the second is I don't know why."

As his lecturing career went on, Twain would develop his platform manner, gradually refining the "Western" persona Harte had defined, with its gritty expostulations that had met with such success in the mining camps of California and Nevada, but would have horrified staid Eastern audiences. He would also attentuate, though not speed up, the drawl that caused one member of a California mining town audience to enquire after a lecture, "Be them your natural tones of eloquence?" Meanwhile, he knew that his audiences loved nothing better than information broken up by earthy stories, delivered in simple, straightforward speech. The verbosity of a Charles Dickens would have seemed false to these miners and laborers. Speaking before them, Twain was able to discourse in a natural, conversational manner, and his descriptive flights of fancy were less hampered by the conventional forms upon which a New England audience would have insisted. By writing as he spoke and speaking as he wrote, Twain unwittingly created a new form of oral literature, one which would ultimately do much to liberate American literature from the almost terminal politesse that was threatening to choke it to death in the period associated with Longfellow, Emerson, and Holmes; and the fresh air of the West was the birthplace of that style.

*   *   *

After finishing up the last of his California lecturing engagements, Twain turned next to Nevada—not without a sense of foreboding, since he had left Virginia City in the spring of 1864, as the saying went, "between two days." As he crossed the Sierra Nevada eastward, he no doubt wondered how he would be received: scornfully, as the evil mastermind behind the "Massacre at Dutch Nick's," or as the returning prodigal, forgiven and welcomed with open arms.

As it turned out, the dark cloud had blown away during the years he had spent in San Francisco, and he was joyfully received by Joe Goodman, Steve Gillis, the *Enterprise* "boys," and the Virginia City populace generally. His lecture at the opera house was attended by a large and enthusiastic audience. As might have been expected, the *Enterprise* had given Twain plenty of advance publicity; more surprisingly, even the rival *Gold Hill News* put in a good word for their former nemesis. (He was no longer writing for the *Enterprise*, so they had little to lose by jumping on the bandwagon and praising him.) Following his lecture and its glowing reception, Twain was so thrilled that he wrote his mother and sister that "even though the flush times are past, and it has long been impossible to more than half fill the theatre here . . . they filled it for me, night before last—full—dollar all over the house."

But it was only after lecturing in Carson City a week later that Twain felt truly absolved of his Sanitary Fund trespasses. He had never been one of that city's favorite people, even before he had presided over the Miscegenation Society scandal and given Carson's fair ladies hell in the pages of the *Enterprise*, but his lecture there was nevertheless well attended. Carson's best citizens assembled en masse to hear Twain, in his own words, "disgorge as much truth as I can pump out without damaging my constitution." All in all, it was a jubilant return to Washoe, and Twain was glad that his years across the Sierra, along with his growing literary reputation, had made him more acceptable to those he had so savagely lampooned.

His original lecture itinerary had included several more towns in Nevada, but shortly after his Virginia and Carson triumphs, Twain had a nasty experience that caused him to cancel the remainder of his tour and beat a hasty retreat home to San Francisco. Following a lecture in Gold Hill, two miles down the hill from Virginia City, Twain and McCarthy were walking back up the hill toward Virginia. It was approaching midnight, and the autumn sky was overcast and dim. They had to ascend and pass through the Gold Hill "divide," which separated Gold Hill from Virginia City—a desolate place, empty of habitation and a favorite haunt of highwaymen and murderers. Two days before Twain's Virginia City lecture, two stagecoaches had been robbed by a gang of road agents two miles from town, and the thieves had made off with all the passengers' valuables as well as the contents of the strongboxes. As Twain and McCarthy reached the top of the hill, the lights of Gold Hill disappeared behind them and a cold, dismal wind began to blow.

Suddenly a dim figure appeared from the direction of Virginia City and came straight at them. Twain stepped aside to let him pass, but he confronted Twain directly, and Twain saw that he was wearing a mask. There was an ominous clicking sound, and Twain recognized the dim outline of a revolver. He was ordered to "stand and deliver," but, as he recounted in *Roughing It*, when he reached into his pockets to oblige, the highwayman ordered, " 'Put up your hands! Don't you go for a weapon! Put 'em up! Higher!' " Twain obeyed promptly. Then the highwayman demanded, " 'Are you going to hand out your money or not?' " Again Twain dropped his hands to his pockets, only to be ordered, " 'Put up your *hands*! Do you want your head blown off? Higher!' "

This went on until Twain was in an extremely agitated state. Finally he beseeched the highwayman and his six cohorts, who had joined their brother in crime, " 'Gentlemen, you see that I've got to hold up my hands; and so I can't take out my money—but if you'll be so kind as to take it out for me, I will do as much for you some—' "

" 'Search him, Beauregard—and stop his jaw with a bullet, quick, if he wags it again,' " said the ringleader. " 'Help Beauregard, Stonewall.' "

Finally, after searching Twain's and McCarthy's pockets and cleaning them out, the chief highwayman said to his fellows, " 'Beauregard, hide behind that boulder; Phil Sheridan, you hide behind that other one; Stonewall Jackson, put yourself behind that sage bush there. Keep your pistols bearing on these fellows, and if they take down their hands within ten minutes, or move a single peg, let them have it!' " Three of the thugs obeyed, and the others, with the leader, disappeared down the road toward Virginia City.

Twain and McCarthy stood motionless by the side of the road with their arms up for a good fifteen minutes, shivering in the chilly wind that was blowing up the divide. Finally they crept down the hill, with Twain expecting at every turn to be blasted by the highwaymen he believed were still lurking behind the rocks and bushes.

The next day, Twain made a discovery: the "holdup" had been a practical joke perpetrated by the incorrigible Steve Gillis, who had played the role of the ringleader. The whole thing had been Gillis's idea of welcoming Twain back to Nevada, complete with the "Southern" references. Worse, Denis McCarthy had been a collaborator. The moment Twain heard this, his mood changed rapidly from shaken and depressed to furious. He had never been able to appreciate a joke if he happened to be the butt of it, and as far as he was concerned, this was the worst joke anyone had ever played on him. It is likely that his anger stemmed from his embarrassment at having shown too much fear and trembling during the "holdup," leaving himself open to ridicule by Gillis and the others.

Twain immediately paid McCarthy off and informed him with considerable heat that he had no further need of his services. Then he cancelled his remaining Nevada lecture dates, including a second night in Virginia City, and returned to San Francisco. He would make light of the whole thing in *Roughing It*, claiming he had never been in fear for his life during the "robbery." But the exposure to the chilly air on the divide got into his lungs, causing him to fall ill with a severe cold, which kept him off the lecture platform for the next three months. The jokers, inadvertently or otherwise, had had the last laugh.

10

A Sourdough in Gotham

After a brief respite, Twain was forced by financial necessity to take to the public platform once more. He chose the Sandwich Islands as his topic, since it had served him so well previously. News stories about his bogus "holdup" had been appearing in San Francisco and Nevada papers, meanwhile, and there were cynical observers who suspected that Twain had actually staged the whole business himself in order to pump up publicity for his lectures. A writer calling himself "Sans Souci," writing in the *Golden Era*, summed up this attitude when he theorized that whiskey cost two bits a glass on board a steamship, and that if Twain wanted to accumulate enough money to travel—as he was always threatening to do—then he needed to pack in good-sized audiences.

The size of the audience attending Twain's second San Francisco lecture at Platt's Hall on November 16, 1866, was enormous, an even larger group than the one that had crammed into Maguire's Opera House a month earlier. They gathered to hear what Twain had billed as his "Farewell Benefit," for he was indeed thinking of traveling again, to New York to oversee the impending publication of his "Jumping Frog" book, and then to Missouri. It had been nearly six years since he had seen his mother, sister, and friends in Hannibal. He stated in his advertisement that he planned to sail for New York on November 19.

Despite the large audience, the second lecture, unfortunately, turned out to be something of a failure. The San Francisco papers were fairly uniform in their criticism, complaining that Twain had padded his lecture with tasteless jokes, some of which were so improper that the female members of the audience hadn't been able to laugh at them without compromising themselves. Worse—at least in the opinion of San Francisco's arbiters of taste—the new lecture had shirked education, choosing instead to offer mere frivolous entertainment. He was roundly criticized, too, for an awkward attempt to wrest laughter from his audience by repeating a dull, humorless anecdote about the well-known journalist and reformer Horace Greeley, and stage driver Hank Monk. The story was already old and stale, and hadn't been particularly funny when it was young and fresh, but even though the audience responded to it with sullen silence, Twain insisted on regurgitating the moldy anecdote twice more, until the crowd was finally forced to laugh at it—if only to get the monomaniacal lecturer to stop his horrid repetitions. The whole business was probably much funnier to Twain than it was to his audience.

The bad reviews weren't the worst of it, either. A few days after the lecture, when Twain should have been headed eastward, the bedraggled prodigal announced a rash of new lectures in San Jose, Petaluma, Oakland, and San Francisco again. The proceeds from the "Farewell Benefit" had, it came out, been attached by creditors for unpaid bills in Virginia City and Carson City. Angered and upset by the "holdup," Twain had left Nevada in a tearing hurry, but this was a new wrinkle.

Rather than bow his head abjectly to his critics, Twain came roaring into the circus ring like a lion, advertising that for his San Jose lecture he would demonstrate cannibalism "as practiced in the Sandwich Islands." On the platform he told his audience that he needed a volunteer. If any mother would be good enough to bring her child up to the platform, he would commence with the demonstration. Then he waited, with a solemn countenance, as if he expected some eager "taker" to come rushing up any minute and proffer her baby. This gambit was so successful at eliciting belly laughs from the audience that he employed it consistently in the lectures that followed.

In Oakland, however, misfortune dogged his lecture at College Hall. The printer had gotten the time wrong on the handbill announcing the lecture, resulting in a woefully scanty turnout. Then Twain was kept standing in the wings while a local school band ran through what seemed an interminable repertory of songs. Twain was perhaps beginning to comprehend Prentice Mulford's admonitions about the difficulties faced by a traveling lecturer.

For his final San Francisco lecture, however, things went much more smoothly. The newspapers reprinted a letter to Twain, ostensibly from twenty prominent San Franciscans, asking him to repeat his first Sandwich Islands lecture, which some of them claimed not to have heard. (They tactfully refrained from mentioning the second lecture.) Twain responded—publicly, of course—with a hearty letter naming December 10 as the date. Announcements in the local press mentioned the lecture's salient features, with the addition of "many uncommonly bad jokes." Twain also announced that since this was positively his last farewell benefit, he would close with an "impromptu farewell address, gotten up last week."

The attendance was all that could be expected, and the "impromptu" farewell speech contained enough rousing rhetoric to satisfy the most rock-ribbed city councilman in the dress circle. "I have been treated with extreme kindness and cordiality by San Francisco," Twain said,

> and I wish to return my sincerest thanks and acknowledgements . . . I am now about to bid farewell to San Francisco for a season, and go back to that common home we all tenderly remember in our waking hours and fondly revisit in dreams of the night—a home which is familiar to my recollection but will be an unknown land to my unaccustomed eyes. I shall share the fate of many another longing exile who wanders back to his early home to find gray hairs where he expected youth, graves where he looked for firesides, grief where he

had pictured joy—everywhere change! . . . And while I linger here upon the threshold of this, my new home, to say to you, my kindest and my truest friends, a warm good-bye and an honest peace and prosperity attend you, I accept the warning that mighty changes will have come over this home also when my returning feet shall walk these streets again . . . Over slumbering California is stealing the dawn of a radiant future! . . . California is the Crown Princess of the new dispensation! She stands in the center of the grand highway of the nations; she stands midway between the Old World and the New, and both shall pay her tribute . . . The straggling town shall be a vast metropolis . . . The time is drawing on apace when the clouds shall pass away from your firmament, and a splendid prosperity shall descend like a glory upon the whole land!

I am bidding the old city and my old friends a kind, but not a sad farewell, for I know that when I see this home again, the changes that will have been wrought upon it will suggest no sentiment of sadness; its estate will be brighter, happier and prouder a hundred fold than it is this day. This is its destiny, and in all sincerity I can say, So mote it be!

The *Alta California* reprinted this farewell speech in its entirety and added that Mark Twain would hitherto be representing the paper as its correspondent-at-large. He would contribute a weekly letter as the spirit moved him, on whatever subject and from wherever location was current. "That his letters will be read with interest needs no assurance from us—his reputation has been made here in California . . . and we feel confident his letters to the *Alta*, from his new field of observation, will give him a world-wide reputation."

The *Alta*'s editors were correct: the letters Twain sent back to them, a few months down the line, when he embarked on the *Quaker City* Holy Land Pleasure Excursion, would ultimately establish his reputation as America's greatest man of letters. But he wasn't quite finished with the West, yet, any more than the West was finished with him.

If Clemens's journey to the West on the Overland stage had been a rolling feast of wonders, his voyage to New York was a rocking nightmare. Under the most propitious of circumstances, the trip was grueling, involving numerous changes of conveyances, both on sea and across land; but Twain's passage was especially harrowing, for from the very beginning the passengers were dogged by cholera. During the trip, the steamship *San Francisco* was, in Twain's words, "a floating hospital," with new deaths almost daily. The entries in his notebook during the voyage were a litany of sickness and deaths, with observations such as, "Folded his hands after his stormy life & slept in serenest repose under the peaceful sighing of the summer wind among the grasses over his grave."

Death had been Twain's closest companion from his earliest boyhood; one of his earliest memories of his mother had been the sight of her kneeling beside the deathbed of his brother Benjamin, moaning in anguish. Twain's sister Margaret had also died in childhood, and his younger brother Henry, who was his favorite sibling, had died in 1858 as a result of a steamboat explosion. Although Twain was not in the least responsible for Henry's death, he was plagued throughout his life by guilt about it. Now, writing in his notebook about the dead and dying, he found his memory jogged by the strange juxtaposition of death and life, past and present. He jotted down many old memories of his life in Nevada and California: experiences he remembered from San Francisco and Virginia City and the mining camps of the Sierra Nevada. These entries would eventually become part of *Roughing It*.

Twain had time to reflect on these things during the trip, for although he escaped the cholera epidemic, he admitted to having "something worse"—perhaps the recurrent symptoms, resembling those of syphilis, which he had experienced during his Sandwich Islands sojourn. He was reluctant to disclose the nature of the ailment, although it had caused him enough discomfort to make him cancel social engagements in San Francisco prior to his departure for New York. He had hoped the infirmity would clear up by the time he left California, but apparently it only worsened, until he was obliged to remain in bed in his stateroom aboard the steamer *America*, where he relied on the reports of his fellow passengers in writing up his accounts of life aboard ship for the *Alta*.

During the trip Twain made the acquaintance of Captain Edgar Wakeman, the San Francisco seaman who would become one of Twain's most prominent characters. Wakeman was a vigorous, middle-aged man, "tall; large; all brawn, muscle and health; powerful bass voice, deep and resonant." Twain was instantly taken by Wakeman's prowess as a yarn-spinner of colloquial force and rare imagination, and used up many notebook pages reproducing the captain's tall tales and random observations. In fact, Wakeman seems to have been Twain's chief refuge from the horrors of death that engulfed the voyage. In various guises, Wakeman would appear in *Roughing It*, in "Some Rambling Notes of an Idle Excursion," in various drafts of essays and short stories, and finally, in "Extract from Captain Stormfield's Visit to Heaven," which was based on a dream Wakeman would describe to Twain during Twain's last trip to California in 1869.

For Twain, Wakeman was an archetype—the last of the bold, blustering figures he had first met on the Mississippi and had encountered successively in the West. Men like Wakeman were literally captains of their own destinies, transcending the cosmic vagaries of life and death (when the fictional Wakeman visited heaven, he refused to accept the final judgment of God). Twain seems to have transformed Wakeman into a fictional character almost immediately, and he continued to think of him that way, doing the image, if not the man, homage by naming his own last residence "Stormfield." Against the backdrop of death on board the ship heading East, Wakeman came to represent for Twain a force greater than mortality, a blustering sailor voyaging into the seas of eternity.

The personality of Wakeman/Stormfield never changed, but his significance did: by 1905–06, when Twain wrote "The Refuge of the Derelicts," Stormfield had become the captain and protector of a group of drifting, feeble losers—and as their sole source of sustenance, Stormfield was ultimately devoured by those he sought to preserve. It is hard not to think that the seeds of this bleak fable did not lie in the cholera-ridden voyage of late 1866.

*   *   *

On January 12, 1867, Twain sailed into icy New York harbor after spending a harrowing month on his cross-country journey. He was glad enough to be there. The city had been his home for six months in 1853 when, as a greenhorn nineteen year old, he had drifted there from Hannibal to see the World's Fair at the Crystal Palace and, "taking a liking to the abominable place," had remained to work as a compositor. Now, instead of being a stranger to the city, he quickly discovered that nearly every other person he met on Broadway was somebody he had known in San Francisco or Washoe. The celebrity of his "Jumping Frog" story, which had been reprinted far and wide, had marked him as a Westerner in the East. As a roving correspondent for the San Francisco *Alta California*, he still had links to the Pacific coast, and when he ran into friends like Frank Fuller, former acting governor of the Utah Territory, and Charles Webb, ex-publisher of the *Californian*, Twain probably felt as if he were still out West. Many Westerners had come to New York to sell mining stocks or otherwise enrich themselves, and they formed a hearty little community of their own in New York.

Twain had liked Manhattan thirteen years earlier, but this time he had to admit that its increasing urbanization was disorienting. "The town is all changed since I was here, thirteen years ago, when I was a pure and sinless sprout," he wrote in one of his *Alta* letters. "The streets wind in and out, and this way and that way, in the most bewildering fashion, and two of them will suddenly come together and clamp the last house between them so close, and whittle the end of it down so sharp, that it looms up like the bow of a steamship, and you have to shut one eye to see it."

He spent seven weeks covering the city's cultural and social life, high (Henry Ward Beecher's sermons and Anna Dickinson's moral lectures) and low ("The Black Crook," a scandalous burlesque show), and then he threw in the towel. "I have just written myself clear out in letters to the *Alta*," he wrote in a letter home, "and I think they are the stupidest letters that were ever written from New York. Corresponding has been a perfect drag ever since I got to the States."

Twain had originally hoped to peddle his Sandwich Islands articles to a book publisher, but he soon changed his plans after encountering his old Bohemian friend Charles Webb. Webb's own humorous book, "Liffith Lank, or Lunacy," had been published by George W. Carleton just two weeks earlier, and he suggested that Twain approach Carleton with a collection of humorous Western pieces. Twain acquiesced readily; he had been collecting his newspaper articles, or having Orion collect them, ever since he had begun his reporting for the *Territorial Enterprise*, figuring that he might get a book out of them eventually. The success of "Jumping Frog" had renewed his interest in the humorous book project, so when Webb mentioned Carleton, Twain made it a point to see him.

The meeting was not a success. Twain was still smarting many years later when he recalled the circumstances in his *Autobiography*. Carleton, he remembered, "began to swell and went on swelling and swelling and swelling until he had reached the dimensions of a god of about the second or third degree . . . Finally he made an imposing sweep with his right hand which comprehended the whole room and said, " 'Books—look at those shelves! Every one of them is loaded with books that are waiting for publication. Do I want any more? Excuse me, I don't. Good morning.' "

When Twain reported Carleton's rejection to Webb, Webb "bravely said that not all the Carletons in the universe should defeat that book, he would publish it himself on a ten per cent royalty. And so he did."

Since Twain was planning to go to St. Louis to visit his family, he delivered his scrapbook over to Webb and gave him free rein to edit it for publication. He had already compiled a list of selections for the book and had done some minor revisions on the articles by way of softening "coarse" passages and removing or altering Western slang that Eastern readers might not understand. He left for St. Louis on March 3, writing to Webb two weeks later to ask when he planned to publish the book.

Twain's participation in the publication of his first book was minimal. He was too excited by other things: the prospect of seeing his mother and sister, his new career as a lecturer, and something even more thrilling. This was the Grand Europe and Holy Land

Pleasure Excursion, gotten up by a group of "prominent Brooklynites," almost all of them well-heeled and pious. Cultured Americans throughout the country were converging on Europe for the Paris Exhibition of 1867, but the Holy Land Pleasure Excursion, aboard the steamship *Quaker City*, featured the most ambitious itinerary of all: Gibraltar, Marseilles, Paris, Lyons, Genoa, Leghorn, Naples, Palermo, Athens, Corinth, Constantinople, Sebastopol, Smyrna, Palestine, Egypt, Malta, Spain, Bermuda—and these were merely the highlights. Twain, that restless soul, was burning to join them despite his lack of funds and piety. He had no intention of remaining in New York for long, and the Holy Land excursion was to last five whole blissful months.

But there were problems. The fare for the excursion was $1,250, and moreover, applicants for the trip were to be screened by a most pitiless Committee on Applications. Twain figured that with sufficient wheedling, groveling, and urbane bludgeoning he could probably get the proprietors of the *Alta* to pay his passage, but the members of that committee were thoroughbreds of a different color. Among the ranks of the chosen were such of the anointed as Henry Ward Beecher and Lieutenant General Sherman, not to mention forty-five members of Beecher's Congregational Plymouth Church. Nonetheless, as soon as he had returned from visiting his family in St. Louis, the former president of the Carson City Miscegenation Society, assuming boldly, marched down to the Committee's office at 117 Wall Street and forked over $125—the ten per cent deposit required to hold his reservation.

He also began working on the *Alta*'s proprietors, inserting references to the excursion into his articles. "Prominent Brooklynites are getting up a great European pleasure excursion for the coming summer, which promises a vast amount of enjoyment for a very reasonable outlay," he observed in one letter. "The passenger list is filling up pretty fast." A little later he was writing, "I expect to go on this excursion to the Holy Land and the chief countries of Europe, provided I receive no vetoing orders from the *Alta*—and against all such I fervently protest beforehand."

This public display eventually caused the *Alta*—no doubt encouraged by the blandishments of Twain's old friend Colonel John McComb—to wire their New York bureau to "ship Mark Twain in the Holy Land Pleasure Excursion & pay his passage." Twain heard the news when he returned from St. Louis, and immediately hastened to Wall Street to finalize his travel arrangements. There he inadvertently discovered that he had not only passed safely through the penetrating inquiries of the Committee on Applications, but was considered a drawing card for the excursion. "We had to wait awhile, because the Chief manager was not in," he wrote his mother and sister, "& we did not make ourselves known. A newspaper man came in & asked how many names were booked & what notabilities were going, & a fellow—(I don't know who he was, but he seemed to be connected with the concern,) said, 'Lt. Gen. Sherman, Henry Ward Beecher & Mark Twain are going, & probably Gen. Banks!' I thought that was very good—an exceedingly good joke for a poor ignorant clerk."

The excursion was due to depart on June 8. Twain, meanwhile, gloried in dropping in at 117 Wall Street "to inquire how the repairing and refurnishing of the vessel was coming on; how additions to the passenger list were averaging; how many people the committee were decreeing not 'select,' every day, and banishing in sorrow and tribulation." In *The Innocents Abroad*, his later record of the excursion, he wrote,

I was proud to observe that among our excursionists were three ministers of the gospel, eight doctors . . . several military and naval chieftains with sounding titles, an ample crop of 'Professors' of various kinds, and a gentleman who had 'COMMISSIONER OF THE UNITED STATES OF AMERICA TO EUROPE, ASIA AND AFRICA' thundering after his name in one awful blast! I had carefully prepared myself to take rather a back seat in that ship, because of the uncommonly select material that would alone be permitted to pass through the camel's eye of that committee on credentials; I had schooled myself to expect an imposing array of military and naval heroes . . . but I state frankly that I was all unprepared for *this* crusher.

I fell under that titular avalanche a torn and blighted thing. I said that if that potentate *must* go over in our ship, why, I supposed he must—but that to my thinking, when the United States considered it necessary to send a dignitary of that tonnage across the ocean, it would be in better taste, and safer, to take him apart and cart him over in sections, in several ships.

Ah, if I had only known, then, that he was only a common mortal, and that his mission had nothing more overpowering about it than the collecting of seeds, and uncommon yams and extraordinary cabbages and peculiar bullfrogs for that poor, useless, innocent, mildewed old fossil, the Smithsonian Institute, I would have felt *so* much relieved.

With the "Jumping Frog" book scheduled for release on April 30 and the departure of the Holy Land Pleasure excursion set for June 8, Twain had his hands full enough; but he added to the madness by deciding to give several lectures in New York City and Brooklyn. His reasoning was that his reputation and budget would both bene-fit from successful appearances on the lecture platform; expenses for the excursion had been calculated at a minimum of $750 in gold. It wouldn't do for him to undertake the voyage without sufficient wherewithal, and the best way he could imagine of obtaining it was to lecture.

Frank Fuller, whom Twain and his brother Orion had known in Utah, agreed to serve as his business manager for the lectures. To promote interest in the first lecture, at Cooper Union in New York, Fuller and Twain held a prelecture gathering at the Metropolitan Hotel for a large crowd of Westerners, many of whom had known Twain in San Francisco and Washoe. Twain gave forth some im-promptu oratory which convulsed the group, and it looked as though the lecture would be well attended. Fuller also made a special trip to Washington, D.C. to persuade Orion's old boss, ex-governor of the Nevada Territory and now Senator James W. Nye, to introduce Twain during the lecture. Nye promised to do so and wrote Twain a letter praising his Sandwich Islands lecture, which Nye said he had heard in San Francisco. Fuller used the letter for advance publicity and advertising, adding that Nye would be intro-ducing the lecturer.

Twain began revising the Sandwich Islands material immediately, adapting it for his Eastern audience. He was quite concerned that his slangy, conversational style would not go over well with the sophisticated New Yorkers (even if most of the audience turned out to be comprised of Westerners). To compensate, he tried to include as many educational features as he could, to avoid the hated tag of "humorist" being stuck on him and his lecture.

Fuller was concerned about Twain's competition on the night of the lecture. There were at least five or six major events scheduled opposite Twain's appearance, including an "Imperial Troupe of Wonderful Japanese Jugglers" being presented by Twain's Western acquaintance Thomas Maguire at the New York Academy of Music, and "The Black Crook," the notorious burlesque which Twain had reviewed for the *Alta*. As the day drew nearer, Fuller became alarmed at the sluggishness of ticket sales despite considerable advertising in the city's newspapers. He decided to distribute hundreds of complimentary tickets to New York's schoolteachers, ensuring that Twain would have a large and intelligent crowd if nothing else.

The night of the lecture, Twain and Fuller received a severe shock. They arrived at the Westminster Hotel at 7:30 P.M. to collect Senator Nye and escort him to Cooper Union, as had been agreed upon previously. However, Nye was not there. Fuller tried to hearten Twain by suggesting that there had been a mix-up and that Nye would probably be waiting for them at the auditorium, but Twain insisted that they'd been stood up. He implored Fuller to introduce him in Nye's stead. Fuller refused, but offered a better idea: " 'You get up and begin by demeaning Nye for not being here.' "

They jumped in a hack and raced to Cooper Union, only to discover as they approached the auditorium that there was a massive traffic jam for blocks around. "I couldn't believe that those people were trying to get into Cooper Institute; yet that was just what was happening," Twain wrote. He and Fuller squeezed into the hall and Twain wriggled through the crowd until he was finally able to mount the podium. Even the stage was full—"there wasn't room enough left for a child."

Twain's appearance onstage was greeted with a mighty holler from the Westerners in the crowd. Seeming to ignore them, he walked deliberately to the edge of the stage and peered down into the orchestra pit, as if he were looking for someone. Then he returned to the lectern and observed that Senator Nye, who had been scheduled to introduce him, had not showed up as promised— maybe he was lost in the crowd somewhere. The audience was delighted. Twain launched into anecdotes about Nye's territorial governorship that set them roaring with laughter. The lecture that followed was very well received. The audience, Twain wrote, "laughed and shouted to my entire content. For an hour and fifteen minutes I was in Paradise. From every pore I exuded a divine delight—and when we came to count up we had thirty-five dollars in the house."

But Frank Fuller wasn't concerned. He was, Twain recollected, "perfectly delighted, perfectly enchanted . . . 'Oh,' he said, 'the fortune didn't come in—that didn't come in—that's all right. That's coming in later. The fame is already here, Mark. Why, in a week you'll be the best-known man in the United States. This is no failure. This is a prodigious success.' "

Fuller was right. The Eastern press was extravagant in its praise. Offers began to stream in for Twain to lecture elsewhere. In his next *Alta* article Twain dwelled only briefly on his success at Cooper Union, but he did get in a few jabs at Senator Nye, explaining that Nye had not shown up to introduce him. "However, it is of no consequence. I introduced myself as well as he could have done it— that is, without straining myself."

Fuller remained friendly with Twain for many years. Some time after the Cooper Union lecture which kicked off Twain's Eastern lecturing career, Fuller asked Senator Nye why he hadn't come to New York to introduce Twain. Nye responded that he had never intended to introduce Twain because Twain was "nothing but a damned secessionist."

Twain gave the same lecture in Brooklyn shortly thereafter, and repeated it a week later at Irving Hall in New York. Both were well attended, and increased his standing with the *Quaker City* group and, more importantly, with New York and Eastern audiences as well. He no longer needed to fear Eastern contempt for being the prodigal "Bohemian from the sage-brush."

*   *   *

By the middle of April, Twain had seen an advance copy of his *The Celebrated Jumping Frog of Calaveras County, and Other Sketches*, and by the end of the month he was writing in his *Alta* article, "Webb has gotten up my 'Jumping Frog' book in excellent style, and it is selling rapidly. A lot of copies will go to San Francisco per this steamer. I hope my friends will all buy a few copies each, and more especially I am anxious to see the book in all the Sunday School Libraries in the land. I don't know that it would instruct youth much, but it would make them laugh anyway, and therefore no Sunday School Library can be complete without the 'Jumping Frog.' But candidly, now, joking aside, it is really a very handsome book, and you know yourself that it is a very readable one."

However, despite good reviews in such publications as the *Nation*, the *New York Times*, and the New York *Tribune*, by the end of the year *Jumping Frog* had only sold slightly more than 2,000 copies out of the 4,076 printed. Webb did not have enough money to engage in large-scale advertising, and Twain's reputation alone was apparently not enough to sell out the entire printing. He seems to have lost interest in the book almost before it became a reality, having left the bulk of the editing and all of the proofreading to Webb. He instructed Webb "to send such money as may accrue from it to Ma every few weeks," adding, "It may make her rich, or it may reduce her to abject poverty, possibly." The day before he left on the Holy Land Pleasure Excursion, he wrote his family that "As for the Frog book, I don't believe it will ever pay anything worth a cent. I published it simply to advertise myself & not with the hope of making anything out of it."

His mind was not on the book, anyway, for the Holy Land Pleasure Excursion was at hand.

11

The Bohemian and
the Puritans

Two days before the sailing of the *Quaker City*, the passengers were all invited to a pre-excursion reception at the home of Moses Beach. Beach, the publisher and editor of the *New York Sun*, served his seventy guests a lavish buffet on the sumptuous grounds of his mansion in Richmond Heights. As they strolled and chatted amidst the opulent gardens, they saw below them a picturesque panorama of New York harbor, from which they would sail. Despite the fact that the guest list was made up entirely of wealthy, influential people, the rough-hewn and seedy Twain, in borrowed swallow-tailed coat, was the party's brightest spot, enlivening the company, as the *Sun* reported the next day, "with ebullitions of wit." Flushed with the prospect of travel, and, as was often the case, quite impressed with wealth and power, Twain was willing to accept his fellow passengers at face value. "We have got a crowd of tip-top people, and shall have a jolly, sociable, homelike trip of it for the next five or six months," he wrote his childhood friend and former piloting colleague Will Bowen.

At the reception he was introduced to the cast of characters that would people his playhouse for the next six months. Moses Beach, the host, was forty-five, an indifferent journalist but a passionate inventor of printing devices and improvements. As fellow newspapermen, he and Twain might have had something in common, but Twain was soon put off by Beach's piety, a trait he felt was somehow improper in a newspaperman. Then, too, Beach's paper, the *Sun*, was an ideological and political stew, profitable but unfocused. Twain, fresh from stints on extremely well-defined and vigorous newspapers such as the Virginia City *Territorial Enterprise*, probably had little professional or ideological respect for Beach.

However, it was different with Beach's seventeen-year-old daughter Emeline, who was to accompany her father on the excursion. Emeline was fresh, sweet, innocent and naively straightforward— all qualities which Twain almost worshipped in young ladies. They would share a mild shipboard romance, playing chess together during the voyage and continuing to exchange affectionate letters after the excursion. Moses Beach, however, made it quite clear that he didn't want a Western roughneck for a son-in-law, even if he happened to be a celebrated journalist. The romance would never be allowed to develop past flirtation and friendship; if it had, it most likely would have ended in marriage.

The person Twain met at the reception who would subsequently have the most significant impact on his life was also involved, in a genteel way, with journalism. Mary Mason Fairbanks, a motherly woman of thirty-nine, hailed from Cleveland, Ohio where her husband, Abel W. Fairbanks, was the well-to-do publisher of the Cleveland *Herald*. Mrs. Fairbanks, traveling alone on the excursion, was to send back letters to the paper reporting the "pilgrims' progress." Although Twain did not instantly join her inner circle, it was probably inevitable that sooner or later she would become his mother confessor, behavior modifier, and spiritual leader, for he had always appreciated female guidance, beginning with Jane Clemens and going on to include other older women he had known in Hannibal. Twain shortly began calling her "Mother" Fairbanks, and continued to do so for the remainder of their friendship, which would last until her death in 1899. Mrs. Fairbanks appears to have been a bit taken aback at first by the brash, profane Twain, but his charm had won her over by the end of the excursion, at which time she was appointed his editor and censor while he toiled over a huge batch of dispatches to the *Alta* and other papers.

At this point in his life, Twain seems to have felt a strong need for a surrogate family. He was certainly experiencing feelings of guilt towards his own clan, writing to them on the day before the *Quaker City* sailed, "My mind is stored full of unworthy conduct toward Orion and towards you all, and an accusing conscience gives me peace only in excitement and restless moving from place to place. If I could say I had done one thing for any of you . . . I believe I could go home and stay there and I *know* I would care little for the world's praise or blame . . . You observe that under a cheerful exterior I have got a spirit that is angry with me and gives me freely its contempt. I can get away from that at sea." Mrs. Fairbanks would serve as a substitute for his family, as he described in a letter to his homefolk after the excursion. "[Mrs. Fairbanks] was the most refined, intelligent, & cultivated lady in the ship, & altogether the kindest & best. She sewed my buttons on, kept my clothes in presentable trim, fed me on Egyptian jam, (when I behaved), lectured me awfully on the quarter-deck on moonlit promenading evenings, & cured me of several bad habits. I am under lasting obligations to her."

June 8 was the grand departure date. Unfortunately, the excursionists' high spirits were literally dampened by a heavy rain which began to fall the moment the *Quaker City* pulled out from its pier. This misfortune, which prevented the ship's actual departure for two days, seemed to be all of a piece with the tribulations that had beset the excursion prior to the sailing day. Henry Ward Beecher, head of the Plymouth Congregation, had been advertised as accompanying the excursionists, and forty-five members of his flock were to swell the ranks of the "pilgrims" as well. General William Tecumseh Sherman had also been a leading luminary scheduled to take the trip; his endorsement, "Your programme is all that could be desired, and should be adhered to absolutely," appeared in the advertisements for the excursion. But a month before the excursion began, Rev. Beecher formally pulled out amidst rumors that, being a person of sensitive nature, he had found it repugnant to see his name continually used in hawking the excursion. When he with-drew, his forty-five "pilgrims" naturally cancelled also, severely reducing the passenger list and throwing the voyage into jeopardy. Then, when the other excursionists were feeling completely anx-ious and depressed, lo! "Cump" Sherman stepped forward and announced that he had only said the itinerary was excellent and should be adhered to—not that he had any intention of adhering to it himself. In the wake of these disavowals, others rapidly began to desert the sinking excursion, until Twain was left as the trip's sole celebrity. Desperation seized the excursion's promoters, and the dreaded Committee on Applications began to pass less and less select applicants. In the words of one of the travelers, "The commit-tee was only a myth . . . behind the curtain which veiled the imagin-ary faces of its members beamed only the bland countenance of the manager himself, and . . . all the essentials of a good character were covered by the 'twelve hundred and fifty dollars, currency.' " By sailing time the manifest consisted of about seventy passengers; the ship was only about two-thirds full. The vagaries of foul weather on the date of departure seemed somehow appropriate for the excur-sion's reduced and dubious circumstances.

Once the voyage was underway, Twain rapidly began to find numerous people and things to be irritated by. The ship's crew, from Captain Charles Duncan down to his various mates and deck-scrubbers, tended to be officious; almost immediately Twain began to attract icy lectures on the *impropriety* of such recreations as medi-tatively whittling the ship's woodwork with his pocket knife or borrowing an unattended sextant to take sightings with. There were also far too many pious Christians on board, and their nightly prayer meetings were a further source of annoyance. Twain began to question the concept of the voyage being a "pleasure excursion" when he realized that three-fourths of the passengers were between the ages of forty and seventy, with the overwhelming majority of them being religious to boot. By the end of the trip his attitude toward the "pilgrims" would have degenerated until he was refer-ring to the voyage as "a funeral excursion without a corpse."

Twain did find some solace in a group of "wild boys" like himself, with whom he played cards, drank, and exchanged tall tales. Probably his closest shipboard friend was Daniel Slote, whom he had met in New York prior to the trip. "Dan" was, Twain reported happily in a letter home, his "splendid, immoral, tobacco-smoking, wine-drinking, godless room-mate . . . He has got many shirts, and a History of the Holy Land, a cribbage-board and three thousand cigars. I will not have to carry any baggage at all." But although Twain and Slote had been originally paired off as cabin mates, Twain, as befitted his celebrated state, was subsequently assigned to General Sherman's old stateroom, "No. 10," when "Cump" bowed out. Twain's actual "roommate" was Charles Jervis Langdon, a furtive seventeen year old who had been sent abroad by his wealthy father, an upstate New York coal magnate, to prevent him from marrying beneath his class. Charley Langdon tried to hide his youth behind a scraggly moustache and attempts at worldliness which generally fell pitifully flat. He took to hanging around the men's lounge, where Twain, Slote and the other "barbarians" sat smoking and playing poker; one day he ventured to criticize Twain over his shoulder for a questionable play. Twain peered up at him with an expression of mild surprise and then drawled, "Young man, there's a prayer meeting forward in the dining saloon and they need you there." Nonetheless, despite the disparity in their ages and backgrounds, the two grew friendly; probably Charley reminded Twain of himself in his "cub" pilot days, especially when it came out that the feckless lad had left home without a passport. (More significantly, some three years later Langdon would become Twain's brother-in-law.)

As the trip progressed, the irritations increased. Charley Langdon had, in his "fearfully green" fashion, made a real nuisance of himself by pestering the more experienced travelers, asking at every possible moment how he was going to know when he became seasick for the first time. Twain, who referred to Charley as "the Interrogation Point" in *The Innocents Abroad*, observed succinctly, "He found out." Langdon wasn't the only sufferer on board. The Atlantic was diabolically choppy, and, as Twain observed in his notebook, "there certainly are more sea-sick people in the ship than there ought to be. I am more than ever satisfied, now, that we ought to have put to sea in the storm of Saturday . . . everybody would have had a fearful four-hours' siege of sea-sickness & then been over & done with it. But alas! we sailed with a bright sky & an untroubled ocean, & so most of the passengers remain half-sick & half miserable, day after day, & they will never be otherwise until we touch land again."

He added, "I have got the bly-ak [bellyache]—& there's 8 doctors on board." It was his old ailment again, driven to a flare-up by the stormy sea and the pitching ship. Still, he did not consult any of the eight physicians, for, apart from his reservations about the nature of his ailment, Twain had never been convinced of the efficacy of conventional medicine. Nonetheless, at least one of the physicians—Dr. Abraham Jackson, the ship's surgeon and later a pioneer gynecologist—would become a close personal friend during the excursion.

But seasickness, prayer meetings, and old fogeys were all eclipsed by Bloodgood Cutter, the excursion's self-appointed poet laureate (or "Poet Lariat," as Twain referred to him), a "simple-minded, honest, old-fashioned farmer" from Long Island. (The Poet Lariat also happened to be a millionaire.) Cutter was a constant and an indiscriminate architect of banal verses on any and all subjects. He eventually got around to having them printed on sheets of paper with his portrait at the head. "These he wll give to any man that comes along, whether he has anything against him or not," noted Twain. No subject was too trivial for the Poet Lariat; he even versified about his versifying, composing his "Recollections of a Pleasant Time on Deck Last Night," "which Pleasant Time consisted in his reciting some 75 stanzas of his poetry to a large party of the passengers convened on the upper deck." He was impervious to insults and snubs, which he received regularly from the other passengers. For example, Dan Slote held a private conversation with him, observing sarcastically, " 'It must be a great happiness to you to be able to sit down at the close of the day and put its events all down in rhymes and poetry like Byron and Shakespeare and those fellows!' "

173

Responded the poet serenely: " 'Oh, yes, it is—it is. There is no pleasure like it in the world!' "

The simple-minded and self-contained Poet Lariat, for all his complacent idiocy, was only a cartoonish version of most of the other excursionists. One of the other doctors on board, whom Twain referred to as "the Oracle," exemplified the philistinism inherent in the "pilgrims." Twain wrote in his second *Alta* letter that "the Oracle is an innocent old ass, who doesn't know enough to come in when it rains, but who eats for four, and is vulgar, and smells bad, and looks wiser than the whole Academy of France would have any right to look, and never uses a one-syllable word when he can 'go two better,' and never by any possible chance knows the meaning of any long word he uses, or ever gets it in the right place. Yet who will serenely venture an opinion on the most abstruse subject, and back it up complacently with quotations from authors who never existed . . . He reads a chapter in the guide-books, mixes all the facts up, with his miserable memory, and then goes off to inflict the whole thing on somebody as stuff which has been festering in his brain for years . . . We don't mind the Oracle. We rather like him. Brown says Solomon was a fool compared to him. We can tolerate the Oracle very easily; but we have got a poet (Cutter) and a born ass (Charley Langdon) on board, and they *do* worry the company."

For his *Alta* correspondence, Twain had exhumed his old traveling companion Brown to serve as a one-man Greek chorus, commenting, in salty language, on the passengers' foibles. But in addition to embodying those opinions and tendencies which Twain himself represented but felt were too coarse to own up to, Brown began parodying some of the "pilgrims": mangling foreign tongues, trying to get his watch to keep pace with the shifting time zones as the ship crossed the Atlantic, and observing with injured propriety, "I like to see a man eat enough but I *do* hate to see a man sit down and eat a dinner and go out and heave it overboard and come back and eat another like a dog." In the *Alta* articles, and later in *The Innocents Abroad*, where he was referred to as Blucher, Brown represented the brash Westerner who had never traveled before, and whose all-too-American sensibilities were continually colliding with those of the Old World. Most of Brown's comments were, of course, the thoughts or statements of Twain himself—the things he was too polite to say in public. As Twain and his imaginary companion traveled through Europe and the Middle East, finding it shabby and disappointing and not being afraid to say so, they were unwittingly pioneering a whole new view of American travel abroad. Heretofore, American travelers making the "Grand Tour" to Europe or voyages to the Holy Land had been expected to wax rhapsodic over the cultural and historical wonders of the Old World. Twain discovered he didn't feel like waxing rhapsodic, and he ridiculed those of the party who did, irritably and savagely.

As the trip progressed, he found himself growing especially savage toward Captain Charles Duncan, the excursion's organizer. Duncan was a temperance man and extremely religious, and although he was not an ordained minister himself, he lost no time in creating a funereal atmosphere on the ship, organizing nightly prayer meetings and going so far as to post lists of shipboard regulations. Twain resented this puritanical tyranny. He had never minded ministers; in fact, in California and Nevada he had often sought them out because he enjoyed talking with them. But he had no use for puritanism or hypocrisy, and those were qualities he felt that the pilgrims in general, and Duncan specifically, possessed in great measure. In *The Innocents Abroad*, he accused the fervent worshippers of lacking charity.

"The executive officer said the Pilgrims had no charity. 'There they are, down there every night at eight bells, praying for fair winds—when they know as well as I do that this is the only ship going east this time of the year, but there's a thousand coming west—what's a fair wind for us is a *head* wind to them—the Almighty's blowing a fair wind for a thousand vessels, and this tribe wants him to turn it clear around so as to accommodate *one,*—and she a steamship at that! It ain't good sense, it ain't good reason, it ain't good Christianity, it ain't common human charity. Avast with such nonsense!' "

Many years later, in "The War Prayer," Twain would amplify this theme of different factions praying to the same God for the same favor, believing *their* side was the right and justified one and that consequently God must be on their side. The origins of this concept probably lay in the prayer meetings of the *Quaker City* pilgrims.

Twain, however, had his own ideas about how to spend the Sabbath, and it was not on Sunday, or in the "Synagogue" at services. He had written his mother prior to departure, "I and my room-mate have set apart every Saturday for a solemn fast day, wherein we will entertain no light matters or frivolous conversation, but only get drunk. (That is a joke.)"

The ship's first stop was Horta, on the island of Fayal in the Azores, west of the Portuguese mainland. The pilgrims were glad enough to stand on terra firma once again after two weeks of battling the turbulent Atlantic. But although for most of them the holiday was just beginning, for Twain, in a sense, it was ending—now he had to commence his newspaper correspondence. Twain was the only full-time, strictly professional journalist on the excursion; most of the others who were sending letters back to their home town papers weren't being paid for them. Twain had promised to send the *Alta California* fifty letters during the excursion, as well as twenty to the *New York Tribune* and a few to the *New York Herald* as well. This added up to an average of four articles a week for the duration of the trip. The *Alta* had paid him in advance for his correspondence, and if he failed to deliver, he was contractually obligated to repay them the amount of the advance. But although the *Alta* was his bread-and-butter account, the New York papers represented his ticket to a wider audience, so he was probably even more concerned about his articles for them than he was about his letters to the *Alta*. At any rate, he had his work cut out for him, and the "pleasure excursion" immediately became serious business. After three days in Horta the ship moved on, heading for Gibraltar, and Twain locked himself in his stateroom and completed his first *Alta* article. He could not have mailed it from the Azores, as the mail service there was primitive, consisting of a monthly packet from Boston and another from Lisbon. But he took advantage of the dull six-day run from the

Azores to Gibraltar to polish up his prose. At one point he became so bored he apparently led one of the ship's evening prayer meetings. Everyone on board was seasick and even Twain claimed he didn't feel "very bright," although his self-prescribed treatment for it was to stay up all night drinking bourbon and playing dominoes with the ship's purser, Mr. Vail.

The *Quaker City*'s entrance into the harbor at Gibraltar was supposed to have been an event of great pomp and circumstance, with a twenty-one-gun salute from the Gibraltar fortress, a mass parade by the soldiers of the British garrison, and an evening illumination of the galleries in the Rock of Gibraltar. But these festivities had been intended to impress General Sherman, not the ordinary mortals on board the ship, and since Sherman was not on hand to be impressed, the pomp was accordingly withheld. After experiencing an initial feeling of awe at the ruggedness of the Rock, the pilgrims rapidly descended into boredom and were quite pleased to leave Gibraltar and move on to more exciting destinations.

Twain's next stop was Tangier. Leaving the *Quaker City*, he and Dan Slote, along with Dr. Jackson and some of the other "wild boys," took a steamer across the Strait of Gibraltar, despite dire warnings of Riffian bandits, dirt, and debauchery. And he was well rewarded for his effrontery. "Tangier is the spot we have been longing for all the time," he said in his *Alta* letter. "Everywhere else one finds foreign-looking things and people, but always with things and people intermixed that we were familiar with before, and so the novelty of the situation lost a deal of its force. We wanted something thoroughly and uncompromisingly foreign . . . foreign inside out and all around—nothing anywhere about it to dilute its foreignness . . . and lo! in Tangier we have found it."

The visit lasted two and a half days, during which Twain saw everything of interest, observed the multifarious population—Moors, Jews, Africans, and others—and was able to reach the conclusion that San Francisco's Barbary Coast, whose namesake this was, was aptly named. Along the way Dr. Jackson acquired the nickname "El Tabeeb," which stuck with him for the rest of the excursion. The skirmishing party loaded up on quaint Moorish garments, odd shoes, and a forty-pound haul of dates; the cheapness of things in Tangier was attested to by an entry in Twain's notebook which indicated that the men had spent $4.50 on food during their stay—and $24.50 on hard liquor.

Back on the *Quaker City*, Twain retreated to his stateroom and cranked out seventy-five hundred words on Gibraltar and Tangier to send to the *Alta*. He would make a mail drop when the ship landed in Marseilles, its next port.

From Marseilles, Twain made a brief excursion to Paris. His whirlwind tour of the city was highlighted by the Paris Exhibition, which he quickly realized was far too large to allow him to see it in one day; and by an evening visit to the Jardin Mabille, where he saw *le cancan* danced for the first time and claimed, in his newspaper correspondence at least, to be shocked by it. (His ruffled propriety was most likely literary, since every saloon in Nevada and San Francisco boasted far seamier, if less coordinated, sights.)

The next stop on the trip was Italy. Here Twain discovered that he loved the city of Genoa ("I want to camp here. I had rather not go any further," he wrote) and hated his fellow pilgrims' snobbishness about the "old masters." During the tourists' sojourn in Italy, Twain noted acidly, they were forever going into ecstasies over paintings simply because the paintings were by Titian or Michelangelo, and thus were *supposed* to be great. Twain begged to differ, writing in the *Alta*, "I have got enough of the old masters! Brown says he has 'shook' them, and I think I will shake them, too. You wander through a mile of picture galleries and stare stupidly at ghastly old nightmares done in lampblack and lightning, and listen to the ecstatic encomiums of the guides, and try to get up some enthusiasm, but it won't come." He summed up his Western American attitude by observing, "Maybe [the paintings] were handsome when they were new, but they have got over it now."

Another facet of Italian life that made an impression on him were the "old monkish frauds." Every cathedral, every village church the tourists visited, had its share of holy relics trotted out solemnly by the priests and exhibited—for a fee, of course—to the tourists. "I find a piece of the true cross in every old church I go to, and some of the nails that held it together. I would not like to be positive, but I think I have seen as much as a keg of these nails," he wrote. Just as he questioned the old masters' contributions to aesthetic history, he found these artifacts of religious history a total humbug. He was rapidly coming to the conclusion that Europe wasn't what it had always been cracked up to be.

But if he was disappointed in Europe, he was horrified when he finally reached the Holy Land. In Palestine he found a blighted landscape where poverty, ignorance, and geographical desolation mingled to create an impression of hell on earth—just where, biblically speaking at least, heaven should have been. Under Roman rule, the Holy Land had been cultivated and green, but largely as the aftermath of two thousand years of tribal warfare and disintegration, the desert had inexorably marched in to reclaim the land. Everywhere Twain went, he was faced with a spectacle that was bleaker even than the Great American Desert at its most hostile. Instead of Washoe Indians, he was accosted at every turn by Arab beggars and cripples crying for "baksheesh;" and the religious hucksterism was, as might be imagined, far worse than it had been in Italy. Nazareth, invested with biblical poetry, consisted of "dirt and rags and squalor; vermin, hunger and wretchedness; savage costumes, savage weapons and looks of hate—these are the things that meet one at every step in Nazareth."

Even the biblical place names seemed inappropriate to Twain. He and some of his confreres began renaming them: Jezreel became Logansport, the Fountain of Jezreel was Jacksonville, and in Canaan, the ancient site of the city of Dan was summarily rechristened Dutch Flat. Throughout Twain's *Alta* letters ran a vein of specifically Western humor, as in his "Ancient History of Dutch Flat," where he described the "Character of the Ranch" (the valley of Dan) and comparing the valley of the sources of Jordan to the Washoe Valley in Nevada ("this country reminds me of Washoe all the time," he wrote). "The longest journey our Saviour ever performed was from here to Jerusalem—say 150 miles—about as far as from Sacramento to Carson City, I should judge," he wrote from Capernaum. Obviously, in his *Alta* correspondence he was reporting from the Holy Land to a specifically Western readership, but the parallels were there. Psychologically, in the Holy Land he was reminded of the biblical parable of the Prodigal Son, with which he had always identified, and of the barren lands of Nevada, where he had gone in self-imposed exile.

In Damascus Twain contracted cholera, which sidelined him and temporarily stopped his correspondence. He and some of the "boys" had branched off from the other *Quaker City* excursionists for a rugged caravan trip to Syria, and Twain, already in a run-down condition, had succumbed to the illness. Describing his brief convalescence, Twain said, "I had nothing to do but listen to the pattering of the fountains and take medicine and throw it up again. It was a dangerous recreation, but it was pleasanter than traveling in Syria."

Still ill and shaky, Twain was forced to rise from his sickbed after twenty-four hours and head on to Jerusalem; not doing so would have thrown him off schedule and ultimately make him miss the *Quaker City*. Hiring a donkey and an Arab driver, he forced himself to take in a few sights in Damascus for the sake of his correspondence, but his illness obliged him to give up after two hours. Just before noon he and the others left Damascus on donkey back for Caesaria Phillippi, and the journey was probably the worst one of Twain's life. "It was the hottest day we had seen yet—the sun flowed down like the shafts of fire that stream out before a blow-pipe; the rays seemed to fall in a steady deluge down the land and pass downward like rain from a roof. I imagined I could distinguish between the floods of rays—I thought I could tell when each lot struck my head, when it reached my shoulders, and when the next lot came. It was terrible. All the desert glared so fiercely that my eyes were swimming in tears all the time." He had left his umbrella and sunglasses in the baggage train, which was ten miles ahead of the procession. The only reference to his suffering, however, was an offhanded line in the *Alta* article: "We . . . rode across the Plain a couple of hours and then stopped awhile in the shade of some fig trees to give me a chance to rest." Whatever Twain's other failings may have been, he was certainly not a complainer—a fact which is more than borne out by even a quick perusal of *Roughing It*, in which he stoically endured extremes of climate, loneliness, poverty, and numerous other adversities without comment. Following this horrendous description of riding through a living hell, Twain went on to make sprightly fun, in his *Alta* article as well as in *The Innocents*

Abroad, of the excursion's pilgrims for their ludicrous appearance with their sunglasses and umbrellas.

Jerusalem was a disappointment, as the rest of the Holy Land had been. He was very glad to rejoin the *Quaker City*, finally, in Jaffa (then called Joppa). "I have only one pleasant reminiscence of this Palestine excursion—time I had the cholera in Damascus," he wrote in his notebook, and, "No Second Advent—Christ been here once, will never come again." Nor would Twain himself.

In Egypt Twain encountered some inspiring sights. In Cairo he wrote in his notebook, "Splendid atmosphere. Beautiful Oriental scenery. Naked girls in the streets—finely built." A jaunt to Giza to see the pyramids and the Sphinx left a lasting impression on him; in fact, for Twain, the Sphinx represented the high point of the entire trip. "After years of waiting, it was before me at last," he wrote in *The Innocents Abroad*.

> The great face was so sad, so earnest, so longing, so patient. There was a dignity not of earth in its mien, and in its countenance a benignity such as never anything human wore . . . It was gazing out over the ocean of Time—over lines of century-waves which, further and further receding, closed nearer and nearer together, and blended at last into one unbroken tide, away toward the horizon of remote antiquity . . . It was MEMORY—RETROSPECTION—wrought into visible, tangible form. All who know what pathos there is in memories of days that are accomplished and faces that are vanished— albeit only a trifling score of years gone by—will have some appreciation of the pathos that dwells in these grave eyes that look so steadfastly back upon the things they knew when History was born . . . and passed one by one away and left the stony dreamer solitary in the midst of a strange new age, and uncomprehended scenes.

Although he never returned to the Holy Land, the image of the Sphinx remained with Twain for the rest of his life. Its silent vigil over history, its magnificent loneliness, were attributes which would seem to him, as he grew older and lost nearly all of the people and things he loved most, more and more part of his *own* role as

America's pre-eminent author. He had no way of knowing his future as he stood there musing on the Sphinx, but the statue's strangeness, and its detached wisdom, struck a chord in him nonetheless.

Returning to Alexandria, he made the worst discovery of the trip when he learned that fourteen of his *Alta* letters had not arrived in San Francisco due to the erratic mails. They must, of course, be reconstructed and sent off again, or he would forfeit his contract. He had not kept any copies of the lost articles, so his work would be momentous.

As the *Quaker City*, battling a ferocious storm in the Mediterranean, fought its way toward Sardinia, Twain knuckled under and began to write. He leaned heavily on various guidebooks to stand in for his fading and lost recollections, and when he became especially desperate, he turned to Mrs. Fairbanks, who not only supplied him with missing facts but in turn extracted passages, phrases, or terms she felt were vulgar or "slangy." The material was certainly the weakest of the batch, both in the form of *Alta* articles and in *The Innocents Abroad*. But as a result of this collaboration between Twain and Mrs. Fairbanks, a friendship was forged which would last for the rest of their lives.

Unfortunately, the remainder of the "pleasure excursion" also wound down with a whimper. Quarantine kept the pilgrims from seeing Malta, Sardinia, Algiers, and Málaga, although Twain and some of his companions did manage to squeeze in a whirlwind tour of Seville, Córdoba, and Cádiz.

The last stop on the trip was Bermuda, which turned out to be one of the excursion's most pleasant ports of call. Twain, long remembering the graciousness with which "our friends the Bermudians" received the excursionists, would return to Bermuda in his last days and spend considerable time there endeavoring to regain his failing health.

Leaving Bermuda after an extended stay of five days, the *Quaker City* headed home, pulling into New York harbor and making its last landing at its Wall Street mooring. After more than five months abroad, the pilgrims had returned, more or less intact.

12

The Return of the
Pilgrims

The *Quaker City* arrived in New York on November 19, 1867. Twain spent just one day in the metropolis following the return of the ship; before leaving on the excursion he had received, and during the trip had accepted, a job offer to serve as private secretary to Nevada state senator William M. Stewart in Washington.

The following day, with Twain safely out of Manhattan and safely en route to the capital, an unsigned article entitled "Return of the Holy Land Excursionists—The Story of the Cruise" appeared in the New York *Herald*. It was a savage burlesque, stating that "the pleasure ship was a synagogue, and the pleasure trip was a funeral excursion without a corpse." It went on:

A free, hearty laugh was a sound that was not heard oftener than once in seven days about those decks or in those cabins, and when it was heard it met with precious little sympathy ... The pilgrims played dominoes when too much Josephus or Robinson's Holy Land Researches, or book-writing, made recreation necessary—for dominoes is about as mild and sinless a game as any in the world, excepting always the ineffably insipid diversion they call croquet, which is a game where you don't pocket any balls and don't carom on any thing of any consequence, and when you are done nobody has to pay, and there are no refreshments to saw off, and consequently there isn't any satisfaction whatever about it—they played dominoes till they were rested, and then they blackguarded each other privately till prayer-time. When they were not seasick they were uncommonly prompt when the dinner-gong sounded. Such was our daily life on board the ship—solemnity, decorum, dinner, dominoes, devotions, slander. It was not lively enough for a pleasure trip; but if we had only had a corpse it would have made a noble funeral excursion.

The following day the *Herald* published an errata notice stating that this valedictory had been composed by Mark Twain, whose name had "inadvertently" been omitted, but such an addendum was probably unnecessary. It was the Miscegenation Society episode all over again, with one major difference—this time Twain had left town *ahead* of the howling mob.

The feud between Twain and Captain Duncan would continue for many years. Duncan was heartily disliked by many of the excursionists besides Twain; the pilgrims generally felt he was high-handed, arrogant, and incompetent. Before the excursion was halfway finished, Twain and Duncan were at loggerheads with one another, with Twain accusing Duncan of all sorts of malfeasances and Duncan dismissing Twain as a godless, drunken lout. In lectures about the excursion which Duncan delivered after the trip, he claimed that Twain had been "full of whiskey, or something" when he first appeared to apply for passage, and that Twain had pretended to be a Baptist minister. Twain got some revenge on Duncan in *The Innocents Abroad*, but it didn't quite salve the wound. He followed Duncan's career with bilious avidity, and when, ten years later, Duncan—now an official in the Port of New York—was accused by the Ship-Owners' Association of misappropriating funds and pocketing bribes, Twain gleefully gave a scathing interview to the *New York World* in which he pointed out that Duncan was just being true to form. Duncan promptly sued the *World* and Twain; the case was settled out of court. Five years later Duncan was again investigated, this time by the U.S. District Attorney's office for taking kickbacks from seamen who wanted to ship out of New York. Again Twain spoke out against Duncan, this time in the *New York Times*.

Nonetheless, despite its flaws and drawbacks, the Holy Land Pleasure Excursion proved both valuable and pivotal for Twain. His experiences on the trip provided him with the material for *The Innocents Abroad*, the book which would propel him to national prominence as a writer; and through his acquaintance with Charley Langdon he would meet and eventually marry Olivia, Langdon's older sister. Although his friendship with Daniel Slote eventually degenerated into animosity, partly as a result of mutual business deals gone sour, Twain remained close to Mrs. Fairbanks; at one point he even considered buying into the Cleveland *Herald*, which her husband Abel published. All in all, the "funeral without a corpse" had helped him make inroads into "respectable" society— even if he had discovered firsthand what he already suspected: that "respectable" society was mightily, annoyingly dull, and needed considerable stirring up to make it palatable.

Twain rolled into Washington with grand ideas, as usual: he would make valuable acquaintances among "these old Generals and Senators and other humbugs," as he wrote to his family. He elucidated his aims in a letter to Frank Fuller. "If I stay here all winter and keep on hanging out my sign in the *Tribune* [he had accepted a freelance staff position on the *New York Tribune*, as well as agreeing to send "special correspondence" to the *Alta* and the *Enterprise*, and occasional articles to national magazines such as the *Galaxy*] and getting well acquainted with great dignitaries to introduce me . . . I can lecture next season on my *own* reputation . . . Here in the next six months I will make . . . a *reputation* that will not be as precarious a capital as it is now." He also hoped to use Stewart's influence to obtain a clerkship in the U.S. Patent Office for Orion, who was back from Nevada and languishing as a compositor in St. Louis.

However, having enjoyed several years of total independence, Twain soon began to find his secretaryship irksome. During his first week on the job, he wrote the Clemenses that "things necessarily move slowly where there is so much business and such armies of office-seekers to be attended to. I guess it will be all right. I *intend* it shall be all right."

Despite those good intentions, the position lasted just two months. In "My Late Senatorial Secretaryship," written for the *Galaxy* magazine shortly thereafter, Twain observed, "I held the berth two months in security and in great cheerfulness of spirit, but my bread began to return from over the waters then—that is to say, my works came back and revealed themselves. I judged it best to resign." He went on,

> My employer sent for me one morning tolerably early, and, as soon as I had finished inserting some conundrums clandestinely into his last great speech upon finance, I entered the presence. There was something portentous in his appearance. His cravat was untied, his hair was in a state of disorder, and his countenance bore about it the signs of a suppressed storm. He held a package of letters in his grasp, and I knew that the dreaded Pacific mail was in. He said: "I thought you were worthy of confidence." I said, "Yes, sir."
>
> He said, "I gave you a letter from certain of my constituents in the State of Nevada, asking the establishment of a post office at Baldwin's Ranch, and told you to answer it, as ingeniously as you could, with arguments which should persuade them that there was no real necessity for an office at that place."
>
> I felt easier. "Oh, if that is all, sir, I *did* do that."
>
> "Yes, you *did*. I will read your answer for your own humiliation:
>
> " 'Washington, Nov. 24
>
> " 'Messrs. Smith, Jones, and others.
>
> " 'Gentlemen: What the mischief do you suppose you want with a post office at Baldwin's Ranch? It would not do you any good. If any letters came there, you couldn't read them, you know; and, besides, such letters as ought to pass through, with money in them, for other localities, would not be likely to *get* through, you must perceive at once; and that would make trouble for us all. No, don't bother about a post office in your camp. I have your best interests at heart, and feel that it would only be an ornamental folly. What you want is a nice jail, you know—a nice, substantial jail and a free school. These will be a

lasting benefit to you. These will make you really contented and happy. I will move in the matter at once.

"'Very truly, etc.,
MARK TWAIN,
For James W. N——, U.S. Senator.'"

Although this account contained some exaggerations and modifications (including the nice touch of substituting the name of James W. Nye for that of William Stewart, as payment for Nye's failure to appear to introduce Twain at Cooper Union the year before), the essence of it was probably true enough. Twain was too independent to serve as anyone's amanuensis. In his *Reminiscences*, Stewart recalled Twain with considerable rancor, describing him as

> a very disreputable-looking person . . . arrayed in a seedy suit, which hung upon his lean frame in bunches with no style worth mentioning. A sheaf of scraggy black hair leaked out of a battered old slouch hat, like stuffing from an ancient Colonial sofa, and an evil-smelling cigar butt, very much frazzled, protruded from the corner of his mouth. He had a very sinister appearance . . . When I first knew him he was a reporter on the *Territorial Enterprise*, which was otherwise a very reputable paper . . . He went around putting things in the paper about people, stirring up trouble. He did not care whether the things he wrote were true or not, just so he could write something, and naturally he was not popular.

With the exception of the black hair (Twain's unruly locks were red), there was more than a grain of truth in Stewart's recollection, although his contention that Twain's behavior was sufficiently villainous to cause the senator to threaten his employee with a thrashing seems a little far-fetched. What probably contributed materially to Twain's resignation was the fact that the senator was unable to nail down any appointment for Orion. Twain himself was very popular in Washington, chiefly as a result of his Holy Land letters in the *New York Tribune*, but freeloading relatives were a drug on the market in the capital. However, through the offices of California senator John Conness, Twain was offered an appointment as postmaster-general of San Francisco, and he gave it serious consideration. Despite his desire to ingratiate himself with Eastern publishers and audiences, he still considered the West his home at this point; he had just recently written to Frank Fuller, "I might take a 'disgust' at any moment & sail for Cal." The postmaster-generalship probably made him think of Bret Harte happily ensconced in the Mint annex, turning out literature to his heart's content without the stress and strain of constant newspaper and magazine correspondence, or the dreary travels of the public lecturer. However, thoughts of his unsatisfactory relationship with Senator Stewart made him finally decide to pass on the position. As a result of his popularity in Washington's social circles, he was beginning to realize that his reputation, as a writer and a lecturer, was growing by leaps and bounds, and that he would probably be able to achieve national success on his own terms, if he could just hold out a while longer.

The realization was complete when he received a letter on December 1 from Elisha Bliss, Jr., head editor of the American Publishing Company in Hartford, Connecticut. "We are desirous of obtaining from you a work of some kind, perhaps compiled from your letters from the past, etc., with such interesting additions as may be proper . . . We are perhaps the oldest subscription house in the country, and have never failed to give a book an *immense* circulation . . . If you have any thought of writing a book, or could be induced to do so, we should be pleased to see you, and will do so."

This was a far cry from Carleton's arrogant indifference. Twain immediately wrote Bliss a reply, mentioning his *Alta* letters from the Holy Land Pleasure Excursion:

> The *Alta* has few exchanges in the East, and I suppose scarcely any of these letters have been copied on this side of the Rocky Mountains. I could weed them of their chief faults of construction and inelegancies of expression, and make a volume that would be more acceptable in many respects than any I could now write . . . If you think such a book would suit your purpose, please drop me a line, specifying the size and general style of the volume; when the matter ought to be ready; whether it should have pictures in it or not; and particularly

what your terms with me would be, and what amount of money I might possibly make out of it. The latter clause has a degree of importance for me which is almost beyond my own comprehension. But you understand that, of course.

Bliss's offer was not the first one Twain had received, but, as he wrote Mrs. Fairbanks, "I like [the offer] of the American Publishing Co., of Hartford, much the best. They publish only by subscription, & by this means gave A.D. Richardson's first book 100,000 circulation & have already given his last one 41,000." These were indeed serious sales figures for the mid-nineteenth century; *Jumping Frog* had only sold about 4,000, a fairly decent number all in all, despite the fact that Twain later claimed he "had fully expected the 'Jumping Frog' to sell 50,000 copies."

After an exchange of correspondence discussing terms, Twain betook himself to Hartford to conclude negotiations with Bliss. Bliss had recently assumed the editorial directorship of the American Publishing Company. He was in his early fifties, a reserved, decorous New Englander of the "cast-iron, or ineffable" type—but the American Publishing Company's board of directors viewed him as a particularly reckless renegade, for he had actually suggested the publication of works which contained pure humor without a scrap of instruction in them.

Bliss, who was ill at the time, nonetheless received Twain with enthusiasm. He had been looking forward to making the acquaintance of the author of the irreverent travel letters from Europe and the Holy Land, which he had read in the *New York Tribune*. But when Twain entered the editorial sanctum, disheveled and sweaty from several days of sooty rail travel, the publisher's first impression was one of dismay. Hanging from Twain's mouth was "a pipe of power," as Paine delicately phrased it in his biography. Soon the room was liberally befogged with rank smoke. Twain marched back and forth through the haze, drawling slowly and steadily. Within minutes, Bliss had become convinced that, as great as Twain's travel letters had been, their author was even greater.

Bliss offered Twain two choices: he could accept a flat payment of

$10,000 for his manuscript, or he could have a five per cent royalty on the selling price of the book. He suggested the latter. Although the ten thousand cash was a powerful temptation to the perennially short Twain, he forbore, and chose the royalty—"the best business judgment I ever displayed," he was later wont to observe. He agreed to deliver the manuscript—between five and six hundred pages— by mid-July. Amidst general handshaking, Bliss then offered Twain the run of his house, which Twain accepted gratefully, and apparently enjoyed, although he wrote home, "Puritans are mighty straight-laced, and they won't let me smoke in the parlor, but the Almighty don't make any better people."

Although he was growing tired of Washington, Twain returned there and promptly threw himself into the revision of, and addition to, material from the *Alta* letters. To make ends meet, he also continued to churn out articles for various newspapers and magazines, writing his family at one point, "I have written seven long newspaper letters and a short magazine article in less than two days." By the end of January he had completed several chapters of *The Innocents Abroad*, which at the time he was calling "The New Pilgrim's Progress." At this point the San Francisco postmaster job was again waved before him; Senator Conness claimed he could virtually guarantee the Senate's confirmation of the post. But, as Twain wrote home, "It was a great temptation, but it would render it impossible to fill my book contract, and I had to drop the idea . . . And besides I did not *want* the office."

Then devastation arrived by telegraph. Joseph Goodman warned Twain from Nevada that the *Alta California* had copyrighted Twain's *Quaker City* correspondence, and that the paper now intended to bring out its own book containing the material. Twain remonstrated by telegraph and mail, and finally the *Alta* responded, offering Twain a share of the royalties but refusing to give up the copyright. Faced with what appeared to be the sure loss of his pet project, Twain wavered. He wrote Orion that "I will bet [the book] never sees the light. Don't you let the folks at home hear that." At this crucial moment, Anson Burlingame, about to be posted as U.S. ambassador to China, suggested that Twain accompany him to the Far East. For a moment, Twain seems to have seriously considered abandoning his literary future and taking off for parts unknown. But, he told Orion prophetically, "We chase phantoms half the days of our lives. It is well if we learn wisdom even then, and save the other half. I am in for it. I must go on chasing them, until I marry, *then* I am done with literature and all other bosh—that is, literature wherewith to please the general public.

"I shall write to please myself then."

Since he was fed up with everything about Washington ("Whiskey is taken into the committee rooms in demijohns and carried out in demagogues," he had observed), he finally decided to return to San Francisco and do battle with the *Alta* at close range; his old friend at the paper, Colonel John McComb, would be his ally. Bliss agreed to issue him an advance against royalties, and Twain used it to his book steamer passage.

In San Francisco, with McComb's help, he succeeded in persuading the *Alta*'s proprietors that they had already wrung full value from his letters, and after Twain agreed to acknowledge them in his preface, the publishers returned the copyright to him.

Bret Harte was just in the process of establishing a new national literary magazine, the *Overland Monthly*, published from San Francisco, through which his frontier stories "The Luck of Roaring Camp" and "The Outcasts of Poker Flat" would subsequently reach a widespread audience in the East. Following a wildly successful lecture in San Francisco on the *Quaker City* trip, Twain pocketed the proceeds ("over $1,600 in gold in the house; every seat taken and paid for before night") and, returning to his old home the Occidental Hotel, settled down to work on the manuscript. For the moment, he was glad to be back in California; he could utilize the literary finesse of friends like Harte in preparing his book. He had not been pleased with the editing Charles Webb had done on *Jumping Frog*, but despite the fact that Harte would exercise considerably more editorial license on *The Innocents Abroad* than Webb did on *Jumping Frog*, Twain seemed pleased enough with Harte's efforts at the time. He later claimed that Harte "trimmed & trained & schooled me patiently until he changed me from an awkward utterer of coarse grotesqueness to a writer of paragraphs & chapters that have found a certain favor in the eyes of even some of the very decentest people in the land." He would write Webb in 1870, after the publication of *The Innocents Abroad*, that "Harte read all the MS of the 'Innocents' & told me what passages, paragraphs & *chapters* to leave out—& I followed orders strictly. It was a kind thing for Harte to do, & I think I appreciated it."

Twain was acutely aware of the fact that his *Alta* letters had been written for a specifically Western audience. His exposure to the upper crust of New England society, both before and after the excursion, had in some ways magnified his old "Sagebrush Bohemian" complex, providing him with more and better targets for social satire but at the same time making him realize that he must tread lightly if he wanted to reach the widest possible readership. The *Alta* material was couched in terms San Franciscans and Nevadans would have no trouble understanding, with constant references not only to local places and things, but composed in an entire attitude that was, for better or worse, Western rather than Eastern. None of the other *Quaker City* "pilgrims" had wanted to reveal their cultural philistinism; they were upper-class, educated, and, hopefully, cosmopolitan in their sensibilities. Twain, on the other hand, writing for his motley newspaper audience of sourdoughs-turned-nabobs, workingmen, and chambermaids, had known he dared not go into ecstasies over the "old masters" nor, indeed, about anything that smacked of Old World convention, lest it be dismissed as pretentiousness or even effeminacy. Deep down, he may have found the task of implanting gentility into his robust material distasteful or downright impossible. He knew he needed help in this area, and Bret Harte was definitely the right man for the job.

In his later days Twain would savagely dismiss Harte's writing as distorted, his characterizations as one-sided, and his transcriptions of colloquial dialect as wooden. These criticisms had objective substance, as can be readily ascertained by comparing "The Luck of Roaring Camp," one of Harte's best short stories, with "The Celebrated Jumping Frog of Calaveras County," one of Twain's weakest. Raw genius is apparent in the latter, in spite of its labored premise and its general air of being a twice-told tale; while, despite the clever and painstaking construction of the former, it feels like the work of an extremely gifted hack, going through the motions to produce an effective piece of writing. Twain would later quote Harte as saying, with a cynical chuckle, that he thought he had mastered the art of pumping up the tear of sensibility. "The idea conveyed was that the tear of sensibility was oil, and that by luck he had struck it."

Harte set to work on the *Alta* letters, suggesting numerous changes, mostly in the form of deletions. He had been charged primarily with reducing the bulk of the finished manuscript, which, at fourteen hundred pages, was considerably longer than it needed to be. In exchange for Harte's editing, Twain allowed him to draw four articles from the material for publication in the *Overland Monthly*.

Harte's editorial input included a recommendation, delicately worded but strongly meant, to strike out a passage on seasickness ("the subject can't admit of the frozen truth without becoming rather broad and Panurge-like," he warned). Another of his suggestions was the elimination of an anecdote about the inhabitants of a Sierra mining camp changing the name of their town from "a Spanish name signifying Devil's Gate" to "Jehovah's Gap." Harte failed to see that such a digression was not gratuitous in the scheme of the book, but, on the contrary, integral to its construction. He was also concerned that the anecdote was irreverent and might harm Twain's reputation among members of the ministry. In view of the fact that Twain was still calling the book "The New Pilgrim's Progress" at this stage, Harte's editorial suggestion seems disingenuous at best.

Despite Harte's best efforts, the finished *The Innocents Abroad* retained many "Panurge-like" statements and observations, and the book's rambling style remained intact. But by following Harte's recommendations Twain perhaps reassured himself that the book's most "unacceptable" material had been removed, rendering it safe for virgin eyes.

*　　*　　*

Twain concluded his final stay in the West with a series of lectures on the *Quaker City* excursion. He spoke in Virginia City and Carson City, where he met with his old friends one last time. By 1868 the flush times of the Comstock Lode boom were long gone, and Virginia City was looking gaunt and worn, her streets no longer thronged with the gay parades of fire companies or with the black ostrich plumes of stately funerals. Twain missed many familiar faces in Virginia and Carson, but the *Enterprise* crew was intact, and he roistered down C Street with them, going from the Sazerac to the Corner Saloon by flickering gaslight in the sharp-shadowed Washoe night, and finally roaring out of town on the tail of a dangling yarn while the boys cheered a hearty farewell. The Comstock Lode was dying, but its creation, Mark Twain, was very much alive.

He gave a final San Francisco lecture, preceded by an advertising campaign that would have been too strident even for P. T. Barnum, in which he made out that the citizens of San Francisco, including "Various Benevolent Societies, Citizens on Foot and Horseback, and fifteen hundred in the Steerage," were imploring him to leave town immediately. Promising that he would depart promptly on July 6 if he were allowed to lecture, he insisted, "I will torment the people if I want to . . . It only costs the people $1 apiece, and if they can't stand it what do they stay here for?" Additional promotional pleasantries included the ostensible warning from San Francisco's chief of police: "You had *better* go." The date of the lecture, at the Mercantile Library, was July 2. On July 6, Twain caught the Pacific mail steamship *Montana* for Acapulco, switched to the *Henry Chauncey* for the trip around Cape Horn, and was in New York by the 28th.

There was one last obstacle on Twain's glory road. In Hartford, Bliss was waging a heated battle with the directors of the American Publishing Company, who were horrified by the frivolity and sacrilege they found in the manuscript of *The Innocents Abroad*. They were imploring Bliss to remove the hideous thing from their catalogue and save them from hell. But Twain insisted that the terms of the contract be honored, threatening that he would sue for damages if they were not.

"That ended the trouble," he recalled in his *Autobiography*, adding, "In nine months the book took the publishing house out of debt . . . and left seventy thousand dollars profit to the good."

It also, needless to say, established Samuel Clemens as Mark Twain and Mark Twain as a household name, ending his decade in the West, but not his identification with that region. He would go on to marry Olivia Langdon, in 1870, and become, in his own words, "a scribbler of books, and an immovable fixture among the other rocks of New England." In 1871, beset by personal difficulties, he would write—perhaps as an escape—*Roughing It*, his version of his Western experiences, and one of his most popular books. Dozens of other Western stories, essays, and fragments, from "The Californian's Tale" to "Extracts from Captain Stormfield's Visit to Heaven," would proceed from his pen during the rest of his life.

He would never return to the scene of his literary and legendary nascence. Years later he would be asked by an old California friend to come West one last time for a visit. By then, Twain was too old, too bowed by the weight of his years, to undertake the journey. But he responded in an unreserved and uncharacteristically emotional manner. "Those were the good old days, the old ones!" he exclaimed. "They will come no more. Youth will come no more. They were so full to the brim with the wine of life; there have been no others like them.

"Would you like to have me come out there and cry?"

Epilogue

Instinctively, as a man and as a writer, Samuel Clemens was imbued with an anarchistic spirit. Presumably this book has demonstrated that such a volatile, independent talent could only have been nurtured on the Western frontier. Twain's legacy—of conversational style, active voice, and subjective organization—went on to influence a generation of twentieth-century American writers, from Jack London to Ernest Hemingway to Jack Kerouac.

One of the most interesting paradoxes in Twain's life was the fact that he could not expect to be accepted as a Western writer until he went East. The failure of *The Celebrated Jumping Frog of Calaveras County* to make an impact on national audiences, coupled with the advice of such mentors as Artemus Ward, Bret Harte, and Anson Burlingame, convinced Twain that he needed to cultivate a more polished surface if he was to reach the masses. Twain followed this advice astutely if not religiously, and he did achieve widespread popularity. But beneath his seemingly respectable exterior as "a scribbler of books, and an immovable fixture among the other rocks of New England," there lurked a dangerous entity indeed: a moralist who had come of age at a time and place when saloons outnumbered churches; a gentleman of letters who had honed his craft in the basement of the *Territorial Enterprise*, or on the scarred surface of a bar-top; a "torchbearer on the instructional platform" who had first practiced his oratory before the "Third House" in Carson City watering holes. Such a figure was bound to blow mid–nineteenth-century literature higher than a powder blast from the bowels of the Ophir mine.

The fallout from that blast has never been cleared away; it is surprising that there is still an atmosphere of controversy surrounding a man who was born a century and a half ago. But then, that was Mark Twain's philosophy anyhow: stir 'em up any way you can—it'll make 'em ask questions later.

Twain's personal and literary style was summed up by Cal Higbie, his old mining compatriot from Aurora. Toward the end of his life the reminiscent Higbie described Twain's antics at a dance held one long-ago night in the Sierra Nevada mining town.

> In changing partners, whenever he saw a hand raised he would grasp it with great pleasure and sail off into another set, oblivious to his surroundings. Sometimes he would act as though there were no use in trying to go right or to dance like other people, and with his eyes closed he would do a hoe-down or a double-shuffle all alone, talking to himself and saying that he never dreamed there was so much pleasure to be obtained at a ball. It was all as natural as a child's play. By the second set, all the ladies were falling over themselves to get him for a partner, and most of the crowd, too full of mirth to dance, were standing and sitting around, dying with laughter.

That is probably as good a description of Mark Twain—man, writer, and Westerner—as any.

Bibliography

Mark Twain, as a giant of American literature, has been the subject of more controversy than almost any other author. From the year 1912, when Albert Bigelow Paine published his three-volume authorized biography, until the present, a steady stream of books, pamphlets, articles, opinions, accusations, and responses have created and sustained a veritable Twain publishing industry.

When I began my research on Mark Twain in 1981, I had read very few of these books and articles. In the process of writing the original book about Twain in California which was the forerunner of the present volume, I made two separate but equally intriguing discoveries. One was that Twain's various biographers had seen relatively little significance in his Western decade; this tendency had begun with Paine, and continued as biographers, generally East Coast–based, chose to focus on other aspects of Twain's life and work. Writers such as Ivan Benson (1938) and Effie Mona Mack (1947) had devoted books to various aspects of Twain's Western years, but they seemed to follow the standard laid down by previous biographers who viewed the period as a brief interlude in Twain's life rather than a key developmental phase. The problem can be traced back to Twain's own reluctance to acknowledge his experiences in Nevada and California as anything other than an embarrassing stint of "roughing it"; Paine had obtained the bulk of his biographical material direct from his subject's oral and written declarations, and thus had, unwittingly or otherwise, passed Twain's prejudices along for posterity.

My other realization was that a surprising number of Twain biographers seemed to dislike their subject to one degree or another. Beginning with Van Wyck Brooks, whose *The Ordeal of Mark Twain* appeared in 1920, a number of psychologically oriented writers had proceeded to address themselves to Twain's psyche, ultimately revealing more about their own peccadilloes than their subject's. This trend enjoyed considerable longevity, reaching its peak (or its nadir) with Justin Kaplan's *Mr. Clemens and Mark Twain* in 1966. Without going into the lurid details, I will merely state that Kaplan and Hamlin Hill (*Mark Twain: God's Fool*, 1977) moved me to write the present book.

I also received inspiration from more positive sources. Franklin Walker's *San Francisco's Literary Frontier* (1939, reprinted in 1970) was the book that sparked my interest in the San Francisco Bohemian scene of the 1860s. Although Walker's primary concentration was not on Twain, he was the first to identify him as a central figure in the California Bohemian movement.

Most of the mainstream Twain biographers from Brooks to Hamlin Hill tended to use Freudian analysis, and yet their subject is best understood in political terms. Philip Foner, on the other hand, in *Mark Twain: Social Critic* (1958), analyzed Twain's political and social significance against the backdrop of his times. In my opinion, if a reader could only read one volume of Twain bio-criticism, this should be it—other than the present book, of course.

As anyone studying Twain's life in depth must, I began my research at the Mark Twain Papers at the University of California, Berkeley. This is the key repository of Twain materials in the world. At the time of my initial research, Twain's correspondence was still in its original, often illegible, form; those letters from 1861 to 1866 have since been published as Volume I of *Mark Twain's Letters, 1853–*

1866. Although the printed versions are admittedly much easier to read, they fail to produce the electric thrill that comes from handling an old, brittle piece of paper upon which Twain vented his vitriol to some hapless correspondent.

Very few original copies of the Virginia City *Territorial Enterprise* are extant due to fire and attrition (unlike articles from the San Francisco *Morning Call*, the *Sacramento Union*, the *Golden Era*, and magazines such as the *Californian*, and the *Overland Monthly*, which are readily available on microfilm). For Twain's *Enterprise* articles, I relied upon the texts in *Early Tales and Sketches* (see below), which were gleaned from reprints in other newspapers of the period.

GENERAL

Beebe, Lucius, and Charles Clegg. *The American West: The Pictorial Epic of a Continent.* New York: Bonanza Books, 1989. (History of the American frontier; heavily illustrated with contemporary engravings and photographs. Includes large sections devoted to the Comstock, San Francisco, and Aurora/Bodie.)

Benson, Ivan. *Mark Twain's Western Years.* Palo Alto: Stanford University Press. 1938.

Branch, Edgar M., ed. *Clemens of the Call.* Berkeley: University of California Press, 1969. (A collection of Twain's *Morning Call* contributions.)

California Historical Society *Quarterly*, December 1961. Civil War Commemorative Issue. (Issue devoted to articles about the Civil War in the West.)

Clemens, Cyril. *Young Sam Clemens.* Portland, Maine: Leon Tebbetts Editions, 1942.

Day, A. Grove, ed. *Mark Twain's Letters from Hawaii.* Honolulu: The University Press of Hawaii, 1975. (The original *Sacramento Union* articles Twain sent from the Sandwich Islands.)

Duckett, Margaret. *Mark Twain and Bret Harte.* Norman: University of Oklahoma Press, 1964.

Fatout, Paul. *Mark Twain in Virginia City.* Bloomington: Indiana University Press, 1964.

––––––––. *The Trouble Begins at Eight: Mark Twain on the Lecture Circuit.* Bloomington: Indiana University Press, 1960.

Ganzel, Dewey. *Mark Twain Abroad: The Cruise of the Quaker City.* Chicago and London: The University of Chicago Press. 1968.

Gillis, William R. *Memories of Mark Twain and Steve Gillis*. *The Banner*, Sonora, California, 1924.

Hahn, Emily. *Romantic Rebels: An Informal History of Bohemianism in America*. Boston and Cambridge: Houghton Mifflin Company and The Riverside Press, 1967. (Colorful overview of American Bohemianism from its beginnings through the 1960s; contains material on Ada Menken, as well as on Twain and Ina Coolbrith.)

Hirst, Robert H. "How Bret Harte Edited 'The Innocents Abroad.' " Thesis, University of California, Berkeley (n.d.).

McGrath, Roger D. *Gunfighters, Highwaymen, and Vigilantes: Violence on the Frontier*. Berkeley and Los Angeles: University of California Press, 1984. (Detailed history of the mining towns of Aurora and Bodie.)

Mack, Effie M. *Mark Twain in Nevada*. New York and London: Charles Scribner's Sons, 1946.

Mighels, Ella S. *The Story of the Files: A Review of California Writers and Literature*. San Francisco: World's Fair Commission of California, Columbian Exposition, 1893. (Contains chapters on the *Golden Era* and the *Californian*, and casts some light on the Twain–Coolbrith–Harte triangle.)

Neville, Amelia R. *The Fantastic City: Memoirs of the Social and Romantic Life of Old San Francisco*. Boston and New York: Houghton Mifflin Company, 1932. (A vivid personal recollection of San Francisco during the 1860s.)

Paine, Albert B. *Mark Twain: A Biography, The Personal and Literary Life of Samuel Langhorne Clemens*, Vol. I. New York and London: Harper & Brothers Publishers, 1912.

Rhodahamel, Josephine D. and Wood, Raymund F. *Ina Coolbrith, Librarian and Laureate of California*. Provo: Brigham Young University Press, 1973. (The only biography of Ina Coolbrith.)

Smith, Henry N., and Anderson, Frederick, eds. *Mark Twain of the Enterprise*. Berkeley: University of California Press, 1957. (A collection of Twain's *Territorial Enterprise* writings.)

Smith, Henry N., and Anderson, Frederick, eds. *Mark Twain: San Francisco Virginia City Territorial Enterprise Correspondent*. San Francisco: Book Club of California, 1957. (Another collection of Twain's *Enterprise* contributions.)

Stellman, Louis J. *Mother Lode: The Story of California's Gold Rush*. San Francisco: Harr Wagner Publishing Company, 1934. (A history of the Mother Lode, with a chapter on Twain, Harte, and Jim Gillis.)

Taper, Bernard. *Mark Twain's San Francisco*. New York: McGraw, Hill, 1963. (An assortment of Twain's articles from various San Francisco publications, including the *Californian*, the *Golden Era*, and the *Morning Call*.)

Walker, Franklin. *San Francisco's Literary Frontier*. Seattle and London: University of Washington Press, 1970.